Energy, Education and War

The United States of America through Documentary Films

ドキュメンタリー映画が伝えるアメリカ
——エネルギー、教育、戦争

Yuko Hosokawa and Keith Wesley Adams

KAIBUNSHA LTD
TOKYO

Photo Credits

All photos and images are either Public Domain or Fair Use from the Wikimedia Commons, Free Media Repository unless otherwise mentioned.

The cartoons on pages 8, 10, 21, and 60, as well as the Map on page 3 are originals by Keith Wesley Adams and are reprinted with permission of the author, who retains full rights.

The photos of Osama Bin Laden on page 6 is a Creative Commons Attribution-Share [CCA-S]. Author: Hamin Mir. Date: somewhere between March, 1997-May, 1998. Source: Canadafreepress com.

The image of Geoffrey Canada on page 23 is a CCA-S. Author: Centre for Public Leadership and Tom Fitzsimmons. Date: 20th January, 2011.

The image of the Gateway Church on page 30 is a CCA-S. Author: Jared Stump. Date: 9th September, 2011.

The image of the Fukushima I Nuclear Power Plant on page 46 is a CCA-S. Author: KawamotoTakuo. Date: 23rd June, 1999, 14:09:47

The image of the Indian Point Nuclear Power Plant on page 47 is a CCA-S. Author: Tony. Date: 9th August, 2008, 17:30.

The image of the GM EV1 on page 55 is a CCA-S. Author: Right Brain Photography (Rick Rowen). Date: 29th March, 2011.

The image of the Crushed EV1s on page 56 is a CCA-S. Author: Plug in America. Date: 17th September, 2010.

The image of the Solar Panels on page 65 is a CCA-S. Author: Raysonho@Open Grid Scheduler / Grid Engine. Date: 17th January, 2013.

はじめに

　日本はアメリカ合衆国のあり方に大きく影響を受ける国の一つです。本書は、アメリカの石油戦略と関連する侵略行為、それと深く関わるエネルギー業界と自動車業界、また国民の価値観や生活にダイレクトに影響する教育といったトピックを取材したドキュメタリー映画の紹介と解説です。ここに見るアメリカの教育、戦争、エネルギー政策は相互に関連しています。絶望を感じる部分もあるでしょうが、アメリカは、こうしたドキュメタリー映画が制作され、興業的な成功をおさめて賞をとる国でもある、ということを心に留めおいて読み進めてください。

　まず Get ready with vocabulary で語彙の準備をして本文を読みましょう。予め、章末の注と内容把握問題に目を通して答えを用意してから授業に臨まれることをお勧めします。

　本書の作成を気長に見守ってくださった開文社の安居洋一氏に感謝いたします。また同志社大学の「現代地域事情」講座の受講生の皆さんの感想や意見も大変参考になりました。ありがとうございます。

　なお、イラストや図などはアダムスが、注などは細川が、英文はアダムスを中心に二人で協力して作成しました。

2015 年 9 月

音声ダウンロード(無料)は

http://www.kaibunsha.co.jp/download/16728

音声は上記URLから無料でダウンロードできます。自習用としてご活用ください。

- URLは検索ボックスではなくアドレスバー（URL表示粋）に入力してください。
- ＰＣからのダウンロードをお勧めします。スマートフォンなどでおこないますと、3G回線環境ではダウンロードできない場合があります。

CONTENTS

UNIT 1   *The Oil Factor: Behind the War on Terror* **(1)** ·············· 1
UNIT 2   *The Oil Factor: Behind the War on Terror* **(2)** ·············· 8
        Directed by Audrey Brohy and Gerard Ungerman, 2004

UNIT 3   *Waiting for 'Superman'* **(1)** ······························ 15
UNIT 4   *Waiting for 'Superman'* **(2)** ······························ 21
        Directed by Davis Guggenheim, 2010

UNIT 5   *Jesus Camp* ·· 27
        Directed by Heidi Ewing and Rachel Grady, 2006

UNIT 6   *The Atomic States of America* **(1)** ················· 33
UNIT 7   *The Atomic States of America* **(2)** ················· 39
UNIT 8   *The Atomic States of America* **(3)** ················· 46
        Directed by Don Argott and Sheena M. Joyce, 2012

UNIT 9   *Who Killed the Electric Car?* **(1)** ················· 52
UNIT 10 *Who Killed the Electric Car?* **(2)** ················· 60
        Directed by Chris Paine, 2006

UNIT 11 *The Fog of War:*
        Eleven Lessons from the Life of Robert S. McNamara **(1)** ····· 67
UNIT 12 *The Fog of War:*
        Eleven Lessons from the Life of Robert S. McNamara **(2)** ····· 74
        Directed by Errol Morris, 2003

Appendix ··· 81

Unit 1

The OIL factor:
Behind the War on Terror <1>

　映画 *The Oil factor: Behind the War on Terror*（2004）は21世紀の石油をめぐるアメリカの動きを暴いている。その動きは当然ながら、「石油の世紀」とされる20世紀の延長にある。

　石油は世界を動かしてきた。第一次世界大戦で石油を燃料としたイギリス軍が、石炭を燃料としたドイツ軍を破り、またガソリン車の普及で石油の需要が世界に拡大することが予見されて以来、石油というエネルギーは国際関係の大きな要となってきた。ペルシャ（イラン）とアラブ（中東）、ロシアや中南米、そしてアメリカの油田は国内外の利権を生み、提携や対立を表面化させ、また欧州連合は、第二次世界大戦後に、エネルギーが戦争の主要因となったことへの反省に立つエネルギー協力機構として始まっている。近年アメリカが自国に埋蔵されるシェール・オイル生産のコストをさげつつあることは、中東や南米の産油国への一定の圧力となり、逆にOPECが生産調整で原油の値段を上昇させなかったのはシェール・オイルへしかけた価格競争とも見られる。

　英石油大手BPが2015年6月に発表した統計によると、2014年の米国の石油生産量は前年比15.9%増の日量1164万4000バレル。シェール・オイル増産により2012年以降3年連続で前年比日量100万バレル以上の増加という世界史上最大の増産記録となり、サウジアラビアとロシアを抜いて1975年以来39年ぶりに世界最大の産油国に返り咲いた。

　イギリスが逸早く中国主導のアジアインフラ投資銀行への参加に踏み切った背景に、2015年ロンドン郊外に発見された油田の存在があると見る向きもある。また2015年イランは一定レベルの核査察を受け入れ経済制裁を解かれ、石油の供給量を増やす見込みである。

　今世紀、アメリカは石油をめぐってどんな対外戦略をとってきたのか。

The Oil Factor: Behind the War on Terror (1)

Get Ready with Vocabulary

Ⅰ 日本語に相当する英語を選びなさい。

1. 戦略的な　　2. 侵略　　3. 査察官　　4. 情報　　5. 安全保障

_____　_____　_____　_____　_____

6. 独裁者　　7. 契約　　8. 通貨　　9. 証拠　　10. 略奪する

_____　_____　_____　_____　_____

proof　　　　　intelligence　　security　　　contract　　　dictator
currency　　　loot　　　　　strategic　　　invasion　　　inspector

Ⅱ 日本語に相当するよう、選択肢を使って英語を完成しなさい。

regime　　　　sanction　　　monopoly　　　interest　　　administration

1. 特定の利益集団　　　　　　　　specific ［　　　　　　　　］ group
2. アメリカ合衆国に敵対する体制（国）　［　　　　　　　　］ hostile to the U.S.A.
3. ブッシュ政権　　　　　　　　　the Bush ［　　　　　　　］
4. 経済制裁を解く　　　　　　　　lift ［　　　　　　　　］
5. 合衆国の独占　　　　　　　　　the U.S. ［　　　　　　　］

Reading

The Case of Iraq

After September 11th, 2001, U.S. Forces invaded two countries in the Middle East: Afghanistan and Iraq. The wars were purportedly to combat world terrorism, specifically Al Qaida*. This terrorist group is held responsible for the 9/11 attack on the World Trade Center* in New York City, which killed 3,000 Americans and foreign nationals.

Based on interviews with a wide range of people from leading journalists and human rights activists to U.S. soldiers

Afghanistan は西アジアに分類されることもある
purportedly 「とされる」

nationals 「さまざまな国籍の人々」

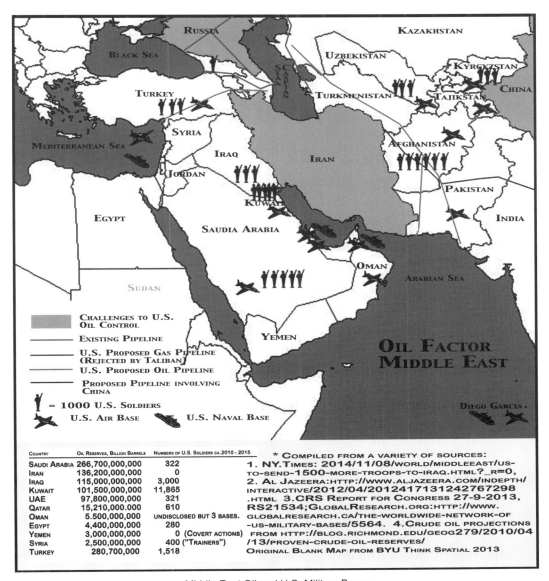

Middle East Oil and U.S. Military Bases

and officers, the movie *The Oil Factor: Behind the War on Terror* (2004) argues the real reason for these wars was strategic control of the world's oil supply by the U.S.A.

Let us look at Iraq first. From the beginning of the U. S. invasion on March 20th, 2003, critics called it an "oil grab," especially as no weapons of mass destruction (WMD), the supposed reason for the war, had been found by the United Nations inspectors. So the argument of the film is not original or surprising. Rather, the movie gives this idea credibility. Even former U.S. defense advisor, Zbigniew Brzezinski appears in the film saying that the fact that Iraq did not have WMD remains a major problem for American credibility in foreign affairs.

An Insider's Testimony

Karen Kwiatkowski, a retired U.S. Air Force lieutenant colonel, claims that the invasion was not based on intelligence but rather on the goals of a specific interest group known as The Project for the New American Century. The written purpose of this think tank is:

Karen Kwiatkowski

1. Embrace American leadership.
2. Increase defense spending.
3. Challenge regimes hostile to the interests and values of the U.S.A.
4. Extend an international order that is friendly to American security, prosperity, and principles.

Among its members are: Dick Cheney, Donald Rumsfeld, and Paul Wolfowitz. All these Neo Conservatives* were in the Bush administration, believe in world domination by the U.S.A., and have close ties to oil and arms companies. Kwiatkowski says that she, as a lieutenant colonel, had a clear sense that part of the job of the pentagon was to fabricate

falsehoods for both the defense department and the media to justify the war by painting Saddam Hussein* as a dangerous
45 despot.

However, as the movie shows, the U.S. government has been friendly with many dictators in foreign countries as long as they supported U.S. interests. Saddam Hussein was one such dictator. Further, Hussein, already beaten down by the
50 first Iraq war and 12 years of sanctions was not posing any threat to the U.S. Above all, there was no connection between Iraq and the terrorist attack on 9/11. But the repetition of Saddam's name in news reports on the terrorist attack led to 70% of Americans believing that he was responsible.

55 ## The True Reasons for the War

Kwiatkowski sums up the reasons for the invasion of Iraq in clear terms: First, geostrategic regional dominance related to energy supplies.

Second, international pressure at the United Nations to lift
60 sanctions on Saddam Hussein threatened the U.S. monopoly of Iraqi oil. If the sanctions had been lifted, European, Russian, and Japanese companies and governments may have gotten contracts for Iraqi oil. America had an urgent need to attack Iraq to prevent foreign companies from settling in the
65 country.

Thirdly, Saddam Hussein had decided to switch the currency used for oil and food exports from the U.S. dollar to the Euro. This would weaken the US dollar and American banks around the world.

70 ## Evidence in the Aftermath Tragedy

Proof of the importance of oil in the conquest of Iraq became obvious soon after the invasion as American soldiers were sent to protect all the oil fields around the country. No soldiers were sent to protect or even inspect Saddam Hussein's
75 nuclear power station where dangerous WMD materials such as uranium or plutonium would most likely exist.

The Oil Factor: Behind the War on Terror (1)

As a result, the nuclear power plant was looted by local people. Unaware of the dangers of radiation, Iraqi farmers dumped the waste and used the barrels for drinking water. Only the intervention of Greenpeace to save their lives brought world attention to the dangers and unprotected reality of the nuclear power plant. Greenpeace collected all the contaminated barrels by trading them with new, clean water barrels. In face of the total lack of concern for the nuclear power station, the rapid protection of the oil fields seems overwhelming evidence of the true reason for the war.

Greenpeace 「グリーンピース」国際環境 NGO

contaminated barrel 「汚染された樽」

Al Qaida 「アル・カーイダ」
　スンニ派イスラム教徒を中心とする、米国に強く反対する組織。幅広いイスラム教過激派テログループに資金を与えて後方支援をし、訓練を施している。アル・カーイダの精神的指導者ウサマ・ビン・ラーディンが財力を用いて初期の反米闘争の組織を起ち上げ、イスラム神学者アイマン・ザワーヒリーが思想と理論の宣伝を担った。ビン・ラーディンがアメリカ政府に殺害されたあと、影響力を維持するまとまった組織として活動しているかどうかは不明。

Osama bin Laden

the 9/11 attack on the World Trade Center 「9・11 ワールド・トレード・センタービル旅客機突入事件」
　2001年9月11日のアメリカ同時多発テロ事件では、アメリカン航空11便がハイジャックされてニューヨークのワールド・トレード・センター北棟に突入した。前年ジョージW.ブッシュが勝利した大統領選は大規模な混乱のため選挙そのものの正当性への議論があり、事件直前、大統領の支持率は50%を切っていた。テロは大統領就任後の初めての大きな事件としてその指導力が国民の注目を浴びることとなり、事件直後には国民の支持率は史上最高の9割に達した。

Neo Conservatives 「ネオ・コンサーバティブ」「ネオコン」
　ここでは特にレーガン政権時代に台頭してきた新保守主義者を指す。本来、保守主義者は、伝統的な価値観、信条などを守り、外交的には孤立主義的だが、ネオコンは米国の価値観や民主主義などを海外、特に非西欧社会に「移植」しようとする。自国に対する脅威（テロや大量破壊兵器など）が想定できる場合にはアメリカ単独でも軍事行動を強行するという意味で極めて「帝国」主義的。その組織的拠点のひとつが、1997年設立の「アメリカ新世紀プロジェクト（Project for the New American Century）」で、当時のチェイニー副大統領、ラムズフェルド国防長官、ウォルフォウィッツ前国防副長官（後の世界銀行総裁）などが名を連ねた。ブッシュ政権には、イスラエル右派の在米ロビー団体であるアメリカ・イスラエル公共問題委員会（AIPAC）がネオコンを送り込んだという報告がある。ネオコンの思想的源流とされるのはドイツ生まれの政治哲学者レオ・シュトラウス（1899-1973）。ナチスの迫害を逃れてアメリカへ渡り、シカゴ大学で1949年から20年間政治哲学の講義を行った。「大衆は物分かりが悪いので、真実は饒舌な嘘をつける一部のエリートによって管理されるべきものだ。民主主義は、脆いながらも無知な一般人の愛国心と信仰心によって守られている。軍事国家だけが人の中にある攻撃性を抑制するこ

とができる。愛国心は、外部からの脅威にさらされる必要があり、もしないならば作り出せばいい」と説いた。ただ、フランシス・フクヤマなど、「イラク戦争侵攻を支持したグループにシュトラウス派はいなかった」ことをあげてブッシュ政権のネオコンへのシュトラウスの影響を否定する学者もいる。

Saddam Hussein　「サダム（サッダーム）・フセイン」

　1979年からイラク大統領。イランとの戦争、クウェート侵攻を強行。1991年の湾岸戦争でアメリカに敗れる。2003年にはイラク戦争で米軍に捕えられ、2006年処刑となる。

Saddam Hussein

　1937年、イラク北部のティクリート生まれ。当時はスンニ派地域でバース党の有力者が多かった。叔父の影響で反英闘争に参加し、20歳でバース党に入党。1959年のカシム大統領暗殺計画に加わるが失敗し、シリアとエジプトで亡命生活を送る。帰国後、地下活動に従事し、1968年バース党のクーデターで、同じティクリート出身のバクル大統領政権が成立すると、翌年32歳の若さでバース党最高決定機関の革命指導協議会の副議長に抜擢。サダムは軍人ではなかったが、巧みに古参党員や軍人を排除し、糖尿病のバクルに替わってバース党の実権を握った。

　「民主化」のポーズも巧みで、バース党独裁色を弱め、国民議会を再開し、またクルド人の自治を認めるなど国民の支持を得た。しかしその権力の実態は、イラン革命の影響を恐れたアメリカの支援を得て石油を国営会社で独占し、その利益をばらまき、軍と治安組織を押さえ、反対派に対しては諜報監視網をめぐらして弾圧する「恐怖の共和国」であった。クルド人やシーア派を化学兵器で弾圧する一方、「サダム病院」や「サダム空港」を建設し、国の隅々まで肖像を掲げさせて、国父として振る舞うのがその手法であった。（酒井啓子『イラクとアメリカ』岩波新書　2002）

　2001年、9/11同時多発テロの後、米ブッシュ大統領は、イラクがテロ集団を隠匿し大量破壊兵器を所有しているとして2003年にサダム・フセインの退陣と亡命を要求したが拒否され、イラク戦争に踏み切った。侵攻した米軍は12月13日にサダムを拘束。裁判は、国際法廷ではなくバグダードのイラク高等法廷で2005年10月から始まった。罪状は、イラン＝イラク戦争中の1982年のドゥジャイル村でのシーア派住民148名の虐殺、クルド人に対する化学兵器による虐殺（アンファル作戦）など全部で13件に上っていたが、2006年11月5日、高等裁判はドゥジャイル村事件のみで「人道に対する罪」を犯したと認め死刑判決を出した。12月26日にはフセインの控訴を棄却して、わずか4日後の30日に処刑した。（『朝日新聞』2006.12.31など）

以下の質問に日本語で答えなさい。

1. 映画『オイル・ファクター』によって、どのような議論が信憑性を得ることになるか。

2. カレン・キアトゥスキーによれば、保守系シンクタンク「アメリカ新世紀プロジェクト」の目的とは何か。

3. カレン・キアトゥスキーによれば、米国防総省はイラク侵攻の正当化にどう寄与したか。

4. カレン・キアトゥスキーによれば、アメリカによるイラク侵攻の本当の目的は何か。3点挙げよ。

5. アメリカのイラク侵攻の目的が石油だったことの証拠と見なされるのは、米軍のどんな行動か。

Unit 2

The OIL factor:
Behind the War on Terror <2>

U.S. Oil Consumption: 20 Billion Gallons a Day, Enough to Circle the Earth

Get Ready with Vocabulary

I 日本語に相当する英語を選びなさい。

1. 需要　　2. 消費　　3. 肥沃にする　　4. 殺虫剤　　5. 冷凍

6. 炭化水素　　7. 必需品　　8. 株主　　9. 幻滅させる　　10. 利益

consumption　disillusion　fertilize　stockholder　profit
pesticide　refrigeration　demand　hydrocarbon　necessities

II 日本語に相当するよう、選択肢を使って英語を完成しなさい。

infrastructure　　brutal　　negotiation　　chemicals　　production

1. プラスチック製品と化学薬品　plastics and [　　　　　　]
2. 食品生産　food [　　　　　　]
3. 社会基盤の修復　[　　　　　　] repair
4. ことに残忍である　exceptionally [　　　　　　]
5. 最後の交渉　the final [　　　　　　]

Reading

The Huge Demand for Oil in America

As of June 2004, oil consumption in the U.S. was 20 billion gallons a day, enough to make a line of oil barrels encircle the entire earth. Only half of this oil is used for fuel. The rest is used for plastics and chemicals.

Michael C. Ruppert, editor and publisher of the web magazine *From the Wilderness*, points out that 1.5 to 6.5 billion barrels a day are used for food production. Agribusiness uses oil at all stages: first, to drive tractors to plough; second, to drive tractors to plant; third, to fertilize with oil based chemical fertilizers; fourth, to water by gas-powered watering systems; fifth, to spray with oil-based pesticides; sixth, to harvest with tractors and combine harvesters; and lastly to transport the food around the world, not to mention refrigeration and plastic packaging. As a result, Ruppert claims, "We eat 10 calories of hydro-carbon energy for every calorie of food!" Because of its oil dependency, retired Brigadier General Pierre-Marie Gallois says, "It is impossible that the U.S. would let itself run out of oil and be dependent on foreigners without a fight."

After the Iraq War, Americans were told that billions of their tax dollars were going for the "rebuilding" of

barrel 「バレル」通常1
バレルは117リットル強
だが、1オイルバレルは
約159リットル
agribusiness 「農業関連
　産業」
plough 「耕作地」

Brigadier General 「准将」

9

The Oil Factor: Behind the War on Terror (2)

Why 1 Kilo of Food Requires 10 Kilos of Oil

UNIT 2

Iraq. But the Iraqi people saw no infrastructure repair.
They had no electricity, water or basic necessities after
the Americans invaded. Even the hospitals were left
ruined and without basics. In reality the money went to
rebuilding military bases and oil refineries by companies
like Halliburton*, whose former CEO, Chairman, and major
stockholder was Dick Cheney*, Vice President under George
Bush.

refinery 「精製施設」

CEO (Chief Executive Officer) 「社長」「取締役」「最高経営責任者」

While cheap Iraqi oil flooded the world market and
undercut the profits of OPEC, the Iraqis themselves faced
oil shortages. Though many Iraqis supported the U.S. in the
first month after the war, they soon became disillusioned and
realized that Americans had come for oil. It is natural new
insurgences and rebellions began within a few months. The
country remains a battlefield today with the Islamic State*
fighting against the U.S. backed Iraqi government, and 3000
redeployed U.S. troops.

insurgences and rebellions 「暴動や反乱」

redeploy （軍を）「転進させる」

The Case for Afghanistan

The reason for the war in Afghanistan seems less clear.
But as the movie shows, while Afghanistan itself has little oil,
the surrounding countries, Uzbekistan, Tajikistan, Kyrgyzstan
and Kazakhstan all have major oil fields. The problem for
the U.S. has been how to get the oil out of these countries.
Furthermore, as these countries are bordered by Russia and
China, the U.S. feared to lose control of these oil fields to
these competitors.

competitors 「競合国」

In the 1990s, the California based oil company UNOCAL*
developed a plan to bring the oil through Afghanistan and
Pakistan. As the United States had helped the Afghani
Taliban* to defeat the Soviet Union, they expected to easily
get permission to run a pipeline through these countries.
However, as the Taliban proved to be exceptionally brutal
against its people, especially its women, women's groups
in the U.S pressured the Clinton administration to pressure

11

the Taliban to improve its human rights record. In response, the Taliban gave the oil pipeline contract to the Argentine company, Bridas. The final negotiation by the U.S. with the Taliban fell through one month before 9/11. One month after 9/11, U.S. Forces invaded Afghanistan.

As if to underscore the oil connection, the man the U.S. government placed in the Afghan presidency was Hamid Karzai*, who had been working for UNOCAL as a consultant. By May 2002, Karzai signed a deal with Tajikistan and Pakistan to run a pipeline through their countries to the Indian Ocean. The reason for the war seems clear. However, now the U.S. government wishes to take the pipeline through Georgia and Turkey, to prevent it from being attacked by China and due to increasing mistrust of Pakistan.

The film thus discloses the oil factor behind the U.S. wars on terrorism, and ends showing us that three fourths of U.S. bases around the world are in oil producing Muslim countries. By the means of war, the movie argues, the U.S.A. has come to control 90% of the world's gas and oil supplies.

Bridas 「ブリダス」2010年5月から株の50%が中国海洋石油総公司の所有
fell through 「失敗に終わる」
presidency 「大統領職」

Georgia 「グルジア」(2015年から「ジョージア」)

U.S. bases 「米軍基地」

Halliburton 「ハリバートン」
　　テキサス州ヒューストンに本拠を置き、120ヵ国以上に事業展開する多国籍企業。石油と天然ガスの探査、および生産設備を製造する、世界最大の資源装置（石油掘削機など）会社。日本支社は新潟市。イラク戦争後の「復興支援」事業や、アメリカ軍関連のケータリングなど各種サービスも提供している。湾岸戦争とイラク戦争で巨額な利益を得た。2015年5月25日には、米同業のベーカー・ヒューズを現金と株式で買収すると発表。買収総額は346億ドル（約4兆円）。売り上げ規模は単純合計で米シュルンベルジェを上回り業界トップの専業企業となる。

Dick Cheney 「ディック・チェイニー」（1941-）
　　ニクソン政権で次席法律顧問、フォード政権で史上最年少（34歳）の首席大統領補佐官。下院議員となり政策委員長や院内幹事を歴任後、ブッシュSr.政権で国防長官、ブッシュJr.の副大統領。上記ハリバートン社の経営に1995年–2000年までCEOとして参加。最大の個人株主でもあり、アメリカ政府と10億ドルの契約がなされた際にはBBCなどのメディアに縁故資本主義が指摘され、不当な戦時利得を得ているとされてアメリカ政府に数百万ドル返還する事になった。また2005年10月から、自らの首席補佐官ルイス・リビーが、イラク戦争に批判的だったジョゼフ・ウィルソンの妻ヴァレリー・プレイムがCIA工作員であると漏洩したとして連邦大陪審によって起訴される。チェイニー自身も情報漏洩に関与していた疑いが持たれている。

UNIT 2

the Islamic State (the Islamic State in Iraq and the Levant, ISIL)

アブ・バクル・アル・バグダディ指揮のもとイスラム国家樹立運動を行う過激派組織である。中核メンバーは、サダム・フセイン政権下の側近や軍上層部と言われる。イラクとシリア両国の国境付近を中心に両国の相当部分を武力制圧し、「カリフ国家」樹立を宣言。ラッカを首都とする。外交関係の相手として国家の承認を行った国家はない。ロイターの記者の 2014 年 9 月の取材によればシリア北東部の砂平原にある町々においては、電気や水を供給し、イスラム銀行、学校、裁判所、礼拝所、パン屋を直接運営しているというが、多くの支配地で恐怖政治が報告されている。SNS や動画サイトなどを利用した巧みな広報戦略で、イラク・イランの周辺地域だけでなく、世界各国から若者を多数兵士として募っている。2015 年 5 月、「有志連合」によるバグダディの負傷が報じられたが、その後 ISIL の活動に大きな影響は見られない。IS については、その中枢はイスラム教徒と無関係でバグダディはユダヤ教徒であるという調査（『パリ八百長テロと米国 1% の対日謀略』成甲社、2015）まであり、実態は不明である。

UNOCAL 「ユノカル」

　1890 年カリフォルニア州に、ライマン・スチュアートら数社が統合して Union Oil Company of California として設立。1901 年にロサンゼルスに本社。1965 年、ピュア・オイル・イリノイズと合併して全米規模の石油会社となる。その後、南部アラスカでの石油生産やメキシコ湾での天然ガス生産において多くの割合を占める会社となり、1983 年に組織を再編、持ち株会社のユノカルが統合会社を支配する形となる。

　他のルートと比べて距離が短く低コストの、カスピ海地域からアフガニスタンやパキスタンを通過してインド洋に出る石油パイプライン建設を目指すのがセントガス・コンソーシアムだが、ユノカルはこの企業複合体を構成する重要企業で、ユノカルのコンサルタントだったザルメイ・ハリルザドは 2015 年 5 月現在アメリカのアフガニスタン大使。セントガスが安全な通過のために払う金額についてタリバンとの交渉が、米政府の硬軟取り混ぜた圧力にも関わらず頓挫したため、パイプラインは建設されていない。一方ミャンマーでは、ヤダナ・パイプライン建設中にパイプラインを守るためユノカルが雇ったビルマ軍が住民に乱暴した、として訴えられている。

Taliban 「タリバン」

　アフガニスタンで活動するスンニ派過激組織。モハンメド・オマルのもと、彼が開いた学校の神学生を中心に 1994 年 11 月結成。タリバンとは「神学校生」の意。カンダハール州都カンダハールを制圧して, 1996 年には首都カブールを陥落させ,「タリバン政権」を樹立した。2001 年 12 月, 米軍主導の連合軍によって最後の拠点カンダハールが制圧され、オマルは, パキスタンのバルチスタン州クエッタまたはシンド州カラチなどに潜伏中とみられるなか、年に数回程度, ムッラー・モハンマド・オマル名の声明が出されている。消息は不明なまま国連安保理の「アル・カーイダ及びタリバン」制裁委員会は, 2001 年 1 月, オマルを制裁対象に指定。タリバンはこの年、アル・カーイダのオサマ・ビン・ラディンを「保護」したとして米軍の攻撃を受け, 政権が崩壊。以降, 駐留米軍やアフガニスタン政府を主な標的としてテロを実行。（公安調査庁ホームページ）2015 年には一時オマルの病死と穏健派マンスール師のトップ就任が報じられたが、直後からの組織の内紛で和平交渉は再び遠のいた。

Hamid Karzai 「ハミド・カルザイ」

　パシュトゥーン人の名門家系に生まれたアフガニスタン人政治家。インドの大学で政治学を学び、1980 年代は米国に滞在。ソ連軍のアフガニスタン侵攻への抵抗で頭角を現し、1992 年ラバニ政権の外務次官に抜擢。1994 年タリバン創設期には一時支持を表明するが、イスラム原理主義が強まっていくことに反発、パキスタンに逃れる。そこで 1996 年頃より、かつてザヒル・シャー元アフガニスタン国王の下で国会議長を務めた父とともにイスラム穏健派を作ってアフガニスタン民族戦線を率い、元国王の復

13

The Oil Factor: Behind the War on Terror (2)

帰を求める運動を展開。1999 年 7 月タリバンとみられる勢力に父を暗殺され、タリバンと対決姿勢を強める。2001 年 9 月米国同時多発テロ事件が発生すると、10 月米国の支援を受けてアフガニスタン入りし前線を指揮。同年 12 月米国の報復攻撃によって崩壊したタリバン政権の後を受ける暫定行政機構（内閣）の議長（首相）に就任。2002 年 1 月東京で開催されたアフガニスタン復興支援会議に出席のため来日。同年 6 月国民大会議で暫定政府大統領に選出。以後、民主憲法の制定や約 300 万人の難民帰還などの実績を上げる。2004 年 10 月同国初の直接選挙を実施し当選、12 月就任し 2014 年まで在任。一方で *The Christian Science Monitor* 誌は "Afghan power brokers" (June 10, 2002) という記事でカルザイとユノカルの関係を報じている。

以下の質問に日本語で答えなさい。

1. 合衆国が大量の石油を求める一要因はその農業のありかたである。それはどのように石油を消費するのか具体的に述べよ。

2. 米軍侵攻後まもなく、どのような状況がイラクの人々を幻滅させたのか。

3. アメリカ政府はなぜ、大油田が見つかっていないアフガニスタンを重要視していると推察できるか。

4. 1998 年、なぜアメリカ政府がアフガニスタン派兵に踏み切ったと推察できるか。

5. 今なぜアメリカ政府は、グルジアとトルコにパイプラインを通そうとしているのか。

Unit 3
Waiting for 'Superman' <1>

かつてアメリカでは肌の色によって大学進学率に大差があった。今も肌の色と貧困の関係が消えたわけではないが、近年はむしろ親が裕福かどうかで大学進学の是非が決まる場合が多い。スタンフォード大学の社会学者、ショーン・リアダンが行った2012年の調査によれば、1960年代以降、共通試験（Standardized reading test scores）の成績格差は白人と黒人という比較では縮まる一方、中層上部以上と低所得者層という比較ではどんどん拡大している。四年制大学を卒業しているかどうかは若者の将来の成功の重要なファクターで、親が貧しいと大学卒というスタート台に立てないことになる。日本でも子供のおよそ16%が「貧困家庭」で育ち、大学進学において不利な状況に置かれているという報告があり、この視点ではアメリカは日本型に近づいているともいえる。

裕福な親は、ともにスポーツを楽しみ、ダンスや音楽のレッスンに通わせ、家庭教師を付け、学校の活動に参加して意見を述べるなど、子供に多くの金と時間をかけることができる。他方、貧困層の親の多くはシングルマザーで、仕事と子育ての両立に苦しんでいる。さらに近年、アメリカの大学の授業料が値上がりし、もはや平均的な中流家庭では、たとえばアイビーリーグの大学に子供をやることは難しい。奨学金制度もあるが、申請手続きそのものが複雑難解で、移民第一世の親の理解などははるかに超えている。

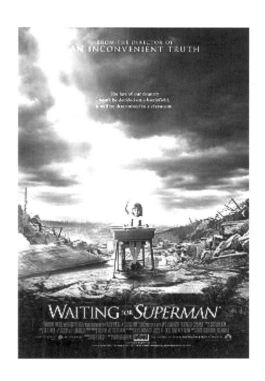

また最近のアメリカの大学入学選抜は、科目の成績のほか、高校時代にした「特別な活動」が審査の重要な決め手になる。スポーツでの活躍のほか、例えば疑似裁判や演劇活動が大学の入試担当官に高く評価されると言われるが、疑似裁判では、週末ごとに親は開催場へ子供を送らねばならず、多くが時間的な余裕のない低所得層には無理である。

Waiting for 'Superman' はそんなアメリカの教育格差の一因である公教育の問題点と、それに取り組む動きをレポートしている。

Waiting for 'Superman' (1)

Get Ready with Vocabulary

Ⅰ　日本語に相当する英語を選びなさい。

1. 失敗	**2.** 調査する	**3.** 最終的には	**4.** 個々人	**5.** 改革者
_____	_____	_____	_____	_____

6. 解決	**7.** 障害	**8.** 自己運営権のある	**9.** 同僚	**10.** 課題を出す
_____	_____	_____	_____	_____

reformer　　　solution　　　failure　　　hindrance　　　colleague
assign　　　　survey　　　　ultimately　　individuals　　autonomous

Ⅱ　日本語に相当するよう、選択肢を使って英語を完成しなさい。

incompetence　　proficiency　　assess　　licensing　　bureaucratic

1. 熟達度　　　　　　　　　　[　　　　　　　　] **rate**
2. 必要を査定する　　　　　　[　　　　　　　　] **the needs**
3. 官僚的な制度　　　　　　　[　　　　　　　　] **system**
4. 資格免許試験　　　　　　　[　　　　　　　　] **exam**
5. 不適切な勤務態度や無能な場合　**case of abuse or** [　　　　　　　　]

16

Reading

The Failure of American Education

Until the 1970s, the United States had the best public schools in the world. Since the 1900s they produced over a hundred Nobel laureates and countless great people from Walt Disney to Steve Jobs, from astronauts to musicians. But in the last 40 years, American schools have declined so that now out of the 30 developed countries surveyed, the U.S. placed 25th in math and 21st in science in 2009. Japan rated 5th in reading, 4th in math and 2nd in science in the same year. The top 5% of U.S. students ranked 23rd out of the 29 participant countries.

The American national average proficiency rate for reading and math remains at less than 40%. In Alabama it is 18%, and 14% in Mississippi. Even in the cultural centers of California and New York State the average is only 24% and 30 % respectively. The area with the least proficiency is Washington D.C. with a 12% reading proficiency rate!

This is ironic since it is the nation's capital, and starting with President Lyndon Johnson in 1965, Presidents Reagan, Bush Senior, Clinton, Bush Junior and Obama, all swore they would be known as "The Education President." Republican George Bush even worked with Democrat Ted Kennedy to fix the education system with the slogan of "No Child Left Behind," but ultimately failed. Bush's project focused on test taking instead of taking time to assess the needs of

President G. W. Bush Signs the No Child Left Behing Act
(Senator Ted Kennedy standing 2nd from left)

each student as individuals, not as numbers. Can American education be improved? The documentary film *Waiting for 'Superman'* (2010) is the story of a few education reformers who try to find a solution to this problem.

Hindrances - Bureaucracy and Teachers

One of the key problems of American education is the overload of bureaucratic systems. There are federal, state, county, city and local levels of bureaucracy that all have different ideas of what education and its standards should be. The state of Illinois alone has 876 school districts. In total, there are 14,000 autonomous school boards in the United States.

Another problem is the teachers' unions and tenure. Originally created to protect teachers, especially female teachers from extremely bad pay, the unions have now become a hindrance. They refuse to differentiate between good and bad teachers. Licensing exams for teachers lack the rigors of the bar that exists in law, medicine, engineering, accounting, and many other professions. All teachers get tenure after two years regardless of performance, and once they receive tenure they cannot be fired, even over cases of abuse or incompetence. A hidden video camera in a public school in Milwaukee revealed teachers reading newspapers while students gambled at the back of the class. These teachers were fired, but their union forced the school to rehire them.

The teachers' unions are among the most powerful lobbyists* in the U.S. They have provided over 55 million dollars to campaign finances in the last 20 years. They protect their colleagues. Whereas 1 out of 57 doctors and 1 out of 97 lawyers will lose their right to practice medicine or law every year, only 1 out of 2500 teachers will ever lose their licenses. The only way they can get rid of terrible teachers is trading them with other terrible teachers from another school.

school district 「学区」

teachers' unions → Appendix 参照
tenure 「終身在職権」

accounting 「会計」

rehire 「再雇用する」

Each school hopes the other schools' worst teachers are not as bad as theirs. This kind of teacher trading is called "the lemon dance" in Illinois, and "the turkey trot" or "pass the trash" in other areas.

Teachers Need Help to Help Students

However, a recent study by the Bill and Melinda Gates Foundation* shows that teachers also need help. In the United States, the development of teaching skills is not systematized in any way. Teachers learn mostly through experience, and they generally report that the training they receive, if they do, is of limited utility in practice. Some teachers master their craft over time, but others merely learn to control a classroom.

The foundation surveyed more than 3,000 American classrooms and found that over 60 % were competently managed, meaning that the students were not unruly and did the work assigned by the teacher, but only 20 % were engaged in ambitious learning that challenged students to think, reason, and analyze texts or problems.

The study suggests that most teachers are neither so bad nor so good. Most are just mediocre and the exceptional ones are few. However, Erik Hanushek of Stanford University points out in the movie that the disparity between competent and incompetent teachers is massive, and has a huge impact on the lives of students. Incompetent teachers will barely cover 50% of required material in a year whereas competent ones will do up to 150%. The gap will be a major determining factor on who goes to college and who does not, and therefore who may get a career with decent pay and health care and who might end up in punishing poverty in the future.

---

lemon dance 「不良品のダンス」lemon は不良品を意味する

utility 「有用性」

mediocre 「並みの」「平凡な」

determining factor 「決定要因」

health care 「医療」米国に公的な医療国民皆保険制度はない

punishing poverty 「酷い貧困」

lobbyists 「ロビイスト」

　　連邦政府、州政府、地方政府、裁判所に影響を与えるために動く特定の主張をもつ個人や団体、ある
いはその請負をする人。多くの企業や利益団体は献金をすると同時にロビイストを雇っている。選挙で
選出された公務員以外がロビー活動を行うときは、連邦ロビイング統制法（1946 年制定）に基づきロ
ビイストとして登録をする義務がある。およそ 3 万人とされ、その中には法案の起草を行う者もいる。
　　「政治家が利益団体や選挙区の利益に沿った政策を唱えるのは理にかなっており、ロビイストはその
手助けをしている」「議員や官僚は、当該案件について充分な知識を持っていないことが多く、専門知
識が豊富な業界側が、接点となるロビイストを通じて情報提供を行うことは必要不可欠である」「議員
や官僚は、当該案件の反対派のロビイストからも情報提供を受けるので、裁判所の対審と同じように機
能している」といった主張がある。その一方、辞任した議員がロビー会社を設立して巨額な利益をあげ
て社会的に有害な利益誘導に繋がるなど、巨額献金と並んでロビー活動の問題は少なくない。ちなみに
ロビー活動が本格化したのはユリシーズ・グラント大統領（在任 1869-1877）の時代である。ホワイト
ハウスでの喫煙を妻に禁止されていたグラントは近くのウィラード・ホテルのロビーで葉巻を楽しむ習
慣があった。オックスフォード英語辞典によれば、大統領がニコチンで上機嫌な時間にこのロビーで陳
情を行うようになったことが "lobbying" の語源である。

the Bill and Melinda Gates Foundation　日本語通称「ゲイツ財団」

　　マイクロソフト会長のビル・ゲイツと妻メリンダが、ビルの父の財団も統合して 2000 年に創設した、
世界最大の慈善基金団体。2006 年にはゲイツ自身に次いで世界 3 番目の大富豪で世界一の投資家とさ
れるウォーレン・バフェットが、ゲイツ財団に 300 億ドルを超える寄附をして規模が倍増。バフェットは、
自分の個人資産の 85% を複数の慈善財団に寄付したが、その 85% 中 83% を、彼自身が率いる米投資会
社バークシャー・ハサウェイの株式およそ 1000 万株の形でのゲイツ財団への寄付に充てた。ゲイツ財
団は国際プログラムでは世界の病気や貧困への挑戦を主な目的とする一方、アメリカ国内プログラムで
は、教育改革や IT 技術に接する機会を提供する活動を行っている。ワシントン州シアトルに本部を置
き、ビル・ゲイツ、メリンダ・ゲイツ、ウィリアム・H・ゲイツ・シニア（ビルの父）の 3 人が共同議長、
ゲイツ夫妻とバフェットの 3 人が理事、マイクロソフトの元幹部ジェフ・レイクスを CEO として財団
の運営にあたっている。

以下の質問に日本語で答えなさい。

1.　過去 40 年間、アメリカの公教育が衰退した結果、読解力と数学の達成度の全国平均値はどうなっ
　　たか。

2.　ブッシュに見られるごとく、アメリカ歴代大統領の教育改革のかけ声もむなしく読解力と数学
　　（算数）の力が低いのはなぜだと言うか。

3.　教育改革を阻む要因の一つに教員組合が挙げられている。弊害の実態を具体的に述べよ。

4.　ゲイツ財団の研究によれば、教師はどんな点で助けを必要としているか。

5.　エリック・ハヌシェックによれば、凡庸な教師と優れた教師の差は生徒の将来にどのように影
　　響するか。

Unit 4

Waiting for 'Superman' <2>

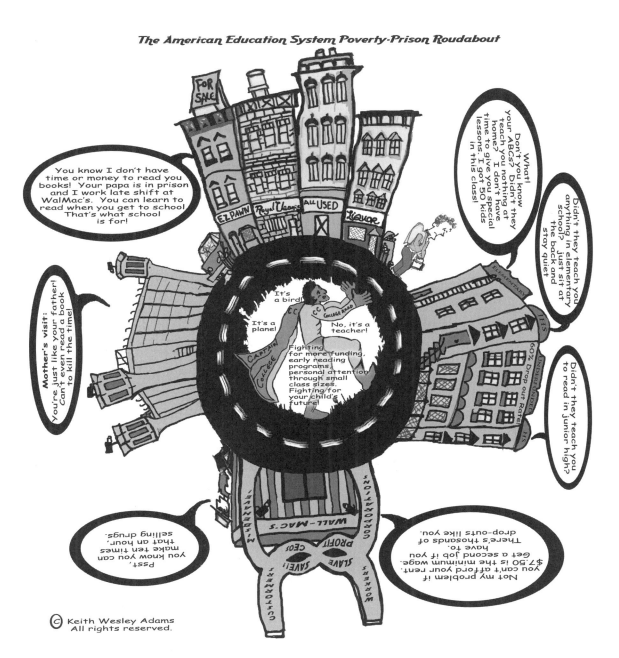

The American Education Roundabout

21

Waiting for 'Superman' (2)

Get Ready with Vocabulary

I 日本語に相当する英語を選びなさい。

1. 悪循環　　**2.** 若者たち　　**3.** 個別指導者　　**4.** 主流　　**5.** 応募者

_____　_____　_____　_____　_____

6. 実現する　　**7.** 籤^{くじ}　　**8.** 競争力　　**9.** 雇う　　**10.** 配分

_____　_____　_____　_____　_____

competitive edge　　vicious circle　　mainstream　　youths　　tutor
applicant　　　　　　lottery　　　　　hire　　　　　allocation　　fulfill

II 日本語に相当するよう、選択肢を使って英語を完成しなさい。

unemployment　　literally　　criminal　　anti-socialist　　workforce

1. 反社会主義的な考え　　[　　　　　　　　] **beliefs**
2. まったく文字通り　　**quite** [　　　　　　　]
3. 教育を受けた労働力　　**educated** [　　　　　　　]
4. 失業率　　　　　　　[　　　　　　　] **rate**
5. 犯罪歴　　　　　　　[　　　　　　　] **records**

22

Reading

Poverty Needs "Culture of Learning"

As a result of America's general anti-socialist beliefs and policies, it is more difficult for students in the U.S. to ever succeed than in any other developed country.

Let us take the example of Locke High School in a poor area of Los Angeles. About 800 out of 1200 students drop out between the 9th and 10th grades. Only 400 graduate. Hence, 40,000 out of 60,000 have not graduated in its entire history. Steve Bar, the principle says that most were pushed through elementary and junior high school without ever developing the basic proficiency in reading and math to get them through high school. Throughout the nation, more than 2,000 such drop-out factories exist.

This is where reformers like Geoffrey Canada* have made a difference. As a child he believed in Superman as some children believe in Santa Claus. When his mother told him Superman is not real, he cried, because he realized there was no one strong enough to make things better. By the end of this documentary movie, however, we see that he himself has proven to be an education Superman.

For Geoffrey, the relation between poverty, poor education and prison is clear. People in poor areas are more likely to drop out; 68% of the prison population is made up of dropouts. Geoffrey realized that many students in poor areas were more likely to know someone in prison than in college. To cut the vicious circle, people in those areas needed positive models and a culture of learning. In response to this fact, he set up an "education pipeline," helping parents in poor areas to put their children on the path to university from birth. In 1990 he established the *Harlem Children's Zone (HCZ)*, which has had such success in helping children that it grew to 11 sites by 1997. In 2009, President Obama announced plans

drop-out factory 「落ちこぼれ生産工場」

Geoffrey Canada

HCZ ＜教育・家族とコミュニティー・健康＞を軸に、貧困の連鎖を断つことを理念に掲げるNPO

Waiting for 'Superman' (2)

to expand it to 20 other U.S. cities.

From Birth to University

Reacting to similar problems for low-income minority children in other cities, David Levis and Mike Feinberg set up a charter school system called KIPP (Knowledge Is Power Program) in 1994. KIPP* schools have longer class hours, including Saturday and summer classes, and the courses are geared to prepare all students for college from the beginning. If students lack reading skills, which form the basis of education, they are provided with individual tutors until they catch up.

The results have been excellent. With the first 1,000 students, the proficiency rate in reading improved from 32% to 60%, and in math from 40% to 80%. In an area where previously only 10% of the youths went to college, 90% of KIPP students proved they were college ready in proficiency tests. In one KIPP school called Summit Prep, 96 % graduated, and they were all ready for college. A neighboring school Woodside, although in a richer area, had a 64% dropout rate and only 3% were ready for college. As Bill Gates says, "they got the culture right, long school hours make it the primary focus of their lives."

Many people used to think the poor simply could not be taught. But like Geoffrey Canada's *HCZ*, KIPP schools have proven them wrong. Now KIPP has grown into a nationwide, open-enrolment college preparatory public school network. There were 82 of them when the movie was shot in 2010, and 162 now, in 2015.

For the Future of America

However, charter schools like KIPP are not yet the mainstream, and do not help everyone. The public school

charter school 「認可公立校」1990年代から増えた、特定の目標を立てて認可された、しばしば12年間一貫の公立学校

the courses 「授業」「講座」

Prep 「大学進学準備の」= college preparatory

system is still failing. One charter school had only 10
places for 135 applicants, and another had 35 places for 767
applicants. Who gets in is decided by a lottery. In the movie
we meet many young people with dreams to become doctors
and teachers, and then we face the fact that the opportunity to
fulfill their dreams is literally decided by chance.

In the United States, schooling is a major factor determining the quality of a person's life. If they win the lottery
and go to a good school, students will prepare for a higher
education. If not, their chances of having a good life greatly
decreases. It is heartbreaking to watch the scene where young
girls and boys lose the lottery.

This education problem will affect America's future.
As Bill Gates says, "You cannot sustain the competitive
edge in a global economy if you do not have an educated
workforce." It is predicted that by 2020, there will be 123
million high skilled jobs available in the U.S., but only 50
million Americans will be qualified to fulfill them. Already
the U.S. hires much of its workforce for hospitals and high
tech firms from India and China despite suffering from an
unemployment rate as high as 10%.

What would it take to make all public schools as efficient
as KIPP schools? Education reformer Bill Strickland points
out that funds allocation is one key factor. It costs $33,000
per year to put a high school dropout in prison, where he
will receive food, health care, security and housing without
paying anything back to society. It only costs $8,300 per year
to put a child through private school, who will then go on to
contribute to society and pay taxes. It is clear that more funds
for education would help break the vicious spiral of poor
education, poor quality of life and criminal records. Neither
the children's nor the country's future should be decided by a
lottery. America cannot wait for Superman forever.

Waiting for 'Superman' (2)

Geoffrey Canada 「ジョフリー・カナダ」（1952- ）
　ニューヨーク、ブルックリン生まれの社会活動家。1990年からハーレム地区の高卒、大卒率を増やすことを目標にしたNPO「ハーレム子ども地区」や、全米を対象としたNPO「子ども保護基金」などに携わる。

KIPP
　合衆国20州と、首都ワシントンがあるコロンビア特別区に160の小中高校を展開。約59,000人の生徒のうち88%が貧困家庭の子どもで、93%がアフリカ系およびラティノ（中南米）系。卒業生の82%が大学へ進学している。（KIPPホームページより）

以下の質問に日本語で答えなさい。

1. 生徒の成功を阻んでいるアメリカ的な価値観とは何か。

2. ロサンゼルス市ロック高校のバー校長によれば、高校の高い中退率のそもそもの要因はどこにあるか。

3. ジョフリー・カナダが言う「悪循環」とは何か。それを断ち切るためには何が必要だと言うか。

4. KIPPはプログラム上、どんな特徴を持っているか。

5. KIPPのようなチャーター・スクールが未だ主流ではない現状を踏まえ、ビル・ストリックランドは、「悪循環」を破るためには何を変える必要があると言うか。

Unit 5 Jesus Camp

アメリカのキリスト教右派の子どもに関わる活動としては、いわゆるメガチャーチが知られる。ショッピングモールのような施設にレストランや託児所まで備えたいわばコミュニティー空間で、格差や競争で分断された人々が集える「場」としての側面も持ち始めている。これまでは宗教保守の牙城だったが、信者が急増することで逆にその政治傾向の幅が広がった。「中絶反対」「同性婚反対」だけでなく、「温暖化」や「貧困」といった問題も重視するようになり、政策的には民主党に接近する動きも見えて、「熱心な信者＝共和党支持」という構図が 2007 年あたりから一部では変わりつつある。しかし映画『ジーザス・キャンプ』が取材するのは、狂信的ともいえる宗教右派による若年層を対象とするマインドコントロール活動で、宗教右派を育てるとされるメガチャーチとも一線を画す。キャンプで子供たちは聖書に書いてあること

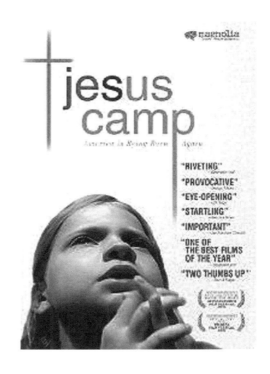

がすべて文字通りの真実だと教えられ、音楽や踊りでトランス状態になり、キリスト教原理主義を信奉するようになるのである。

この映画は第 79 回アカデミー賞ドキュメンタリー映画賞にノミネートされた（受賞は『不都合な真実』）。映画のヒット後、宗教右派に反感を持つ人々によって施設が破壊されることを恐れたキャンプ場の持ち主は、映画の取材対象であるフィッシャー牧師にキャンプ場を貸すことをやめたが、キリスト原理主義そのものはアメリカ社会に脈々と存在する。

The Close Relationship Between God and Guns in the U.S.

27

Jesus Camp

Get Ready with Vocabulary

I 日本語に相当する英語を選びなさい。

1. 洗脳	2. 教え込む	3. 価値観	4. 布教任務	5. 不寛容である
_____	_____	_____	_____	_____

6. 心を病んだ	7. 進化	8. 宣伝	9. 主人公	10. 悔悛する
_____	_____	_____	_____	_____

evolution   brainwashing   values   indoctrinate   propaganda
sickened   mission   repent   protagonist   intolerant

II 日本語に相当するよう、選択肢を使って英語を完成しなさい。

Muslims   medieval   fringe   nomination   global

1. 中世   the [   ] age
2. 地球温暖化   [   ] warming
3. 過激派イスラム教徒   radical [   ]
4. 頭のおかしい少数派の極端論者   lunatic [   ] minority
5. ブッシュによるアリトー判事の指名   Bush's [   ] of Judge Alito

Reading

Brainwashing

The movie *Jesus Camp* (2006) tells the story of how the religious right in America is indoctrinating its children to influence political decisions. Even though the United States
5 of America was founded on the principle of the separation of church and state, the Evangelical Christian* movement is openly against this principle and wishes for the government to be Christian in belief and values.

These are new Christians who claim to be "born again,"
10 that is they are not simply born Christian Evangelicals, but find Jesus "on their own," thus experiencing a "rebirth." They believe they have a mission to spread their religion to "save" others. They are intolerant of other beliefs and openly claim they do not care about the fate of those who
15 do not share their religion. One Evangelical mother in the movie says to her kids, "There are two kinds of people in the world. Those who believe in Jesus and those who don't." Evangelicals see themselves in a culture war to reclaim America for Christ.

20 The movie is non-judgmental. It simply follows the children, primarily of one family, as they go to church and summer camp. But the effect is chilling as we realize how they are being brainwashed. The children's pastor Becky Fischer says, "Give me a child of 7, 8 or 9 years old and what
25 they learn stays with them for the rest of their lives." 43% of Evangelicals become "born again" before the age of 13. In other words, you are more likely to accept this belief system if you are a child and uneducated.

The danger of this brainwashing is made clear at the
30 beginning of the film, when we see the children dancing. The boys are dressed in military fatigues with camouflage paint on their cheeks; the girls are in black, carrying sticks. "It is time

the religious right 「宗教右派」

the separation of church and state 「政教分離」

"rebirth" 「生まれ変わり」強烈な啓示と自己選択を強調する表現

pastor 「牧師」ラテン語の「羊飼い」から派生

fatigues 「作業服」もとは海軍の懲罰雑役用の服

29

for Christ to wash over the earth like the water of the seas," they sing. They are urged to grow to "fix this old sickened world."

What, Where and How the Children "Learn"

What the children are taught is scary: global warming is not important because the temperature is only a little warmer than last summer; evolution is a myth; God created the world 6000 years ago. In short, it is all the creationist and right wing propaganda that is not allowed in American schools. The children can "learn" this because many of them do not go to public school. Evangelicals make up 75% of the people in the United States who home school their children. In this way they try to avoid the influence of science, which is taught in school. To Evangelicals, science is just another "belief system."

The big lessons are taught at a summer camp held at a place, which by an ironic coincidence is called Devil's Lake. Like serfs in the medieval age, the children are scared into believing that the devil is always trying to lead them astray. "At first, it might be only simple joys like having a cute stuffed toy, but the devil will use this to lead you to stop believing in God." Listening to this, they break down in tears thinking of all the sins they have committed – sins like reading *Harry Potter*, whose protagonist Pastor Fischer says would be killed by God in the Old Testament because he is a

Gateway Evangelical Church

A Young Girl Weeping for Her Sins at Devil's Lake Jesus Camp

warlock. They are encouraged to speak in tongues and openly weep, pray and repent.

Campaigning with Bush

Talk radio host, Mike Papantonio, who interviewed Fischer, criticizes her for indoctrinating the children as soldiers for the Republican Party. At the camp, they are led to believe that they are special warriors for Christ and will be a new generation to overthrow evil in their country. "Evil" here means liberal values and "big government".* Fischer claims that she wants children "who will lay down their lives for the Gospels like radical Muslims do for the Koran." This is especially disturbing as it was the religious right that supported Bush for the invasion in Iraq and other regions. Are the children literally being prepared to fight wars for Christianity like crusaders?

Watching from Japan or even from New York City, one might be inclined to write these people off as a lunatic fringe minority. However, Pastor Ted Haggart, the president of the National Association of Evangelicals, announces that there are 80 million Evangelicals in the U.S. "Enough to sway every election," he boasts. "If the Evangelicals vote, they determine the election." And it is not an empty boast. Haggart spoke directly with president Bush every Monday. Evangelicals regard President Bush as a kind of holy man who restored Christianity to the mainstream. Their influence is clear in Bush's nomination of openly anti-abortionist Judge Alito to the Supreme Court in 2006. The children themselves were sent out to Washington to hand out leaflets and spread the anti-abortionist message.

The movie shows how the children, unable to decide and think for themselves, are being turned into a religious political army for the right wing. Evangelicals are brainwashing America's youth to bring down democracy in the name of Jesus, and to go to war and die for him.

---

warlock 「魔法使い」

warrior 「戦士」

crusaders 「キリスト教聖戦兵士」十字軍戦士の意から

Ted Haggart 「テッド・ハッガート」テッド牧師として影響力をもったが、Jesus Camp の上映が始まった 2006 年、男性買春とドラッグ使用の容疑者となり退職
the National Association of Evangelicals 「全米福音主義者協会」

anti-abortionist 「中絶反対主義者」
Judge Alito 「アリトー判事」(1950-) ブッシュの指名により 2006 年から最高裁判事

the Evangelical Christian Movement

　もとは 16 世紀以来の、教会における権威の土台を聖書のみとして、聖書に立ち帰ることを説いたプロテスタントの「福音主義運動」（福音＝聖書の言葉）を指した。ここではアメリカの 1980 年代から目立ち始めた、聖書の一語一句を完全な真理とみなす原理主義に近い人々の活動。彼らは現代アメリカの福音主義者の半数以上にあたるとみられる。たとえば福音主義者の約 6 割が、「アメリカ国民の意思より聖書のほうがアメリカの法に影響力をもつべき」と考えている。また複数の調査で、アメリカ国民の 3 割以上がこれに賛同しているという結果が出ている。つまりアメリカ人の 3 人に 1 人は憲法や民主主義より聖書を政治の指針とすべきだと考えていることになる。また、アメリカ国民の 67% が「アメリカはキリスト教国」と考え、同じく 67% が「アメリカ人の生活にキリスト教がもっと強い影響をもつべき」と考えているという調査結果もある。

"big government" 「大きな政府」

　政府が経済活動に積極的に介入して社会資本を整備し、所得格差を是正して国民の生活を安定させようとする考え方。政府の財政支出が増えるので、税や社会保障費など国民の負担が高くなり、「高福祉高負担」となる傾向がある。公営事業による民間企業の圧迫、政府の規制で市場の自由競争が抑制されるなど、民間経済の活力が奪われる懸念や、また政府支出の増大による財政破綻などの懸念も指摘される。反対に「小さな政府」のキーワードは自由競争と規制緩和であるが、産業や資本の寡占化と格差の拡大と固定化につながる懸念がある。

以下の質問に日本語で答えなさい。

1. 現代アメリカに見るキリスト教福音主義運動は、アメリカ合衆国のどんな基本理念に反しているか。

2. 映画『ジーザス・キャンプ』の最初に見る、子どもの「洗脳」シーンとはどのようなものか。

3. 公立学校では教えられていないことで、取材されたキャンプに参加した子どもたちに教え込まれることとは何か。

4. 新福音主義者たちはブッシュ大統領をどう見ていたか。

5. 新福音主義者らは自分たちを "born-again Christian" と呼ぶ。この呼称の矛盾点とは何か。

Unit 6

The Atomic States of America <1>

　原子力をどうするのか。日本の大きな課題である。

　日本の原子力研究と使用は 1955 年、日米原子力研究協定の調印でアメリカの監視と指導のもとに始まった。正式には「原子力の非軍事的利用に関する協力のための日本国政府とアメリカ合衆国政府との間の協定」と呼ばれるこの協定に基づき、日本原子力研究所に日本最初の原子炉二つが導入された。このとき、アメリカから日本へ、研究原子炉用 20% 濃縮ウラン 235 を 6kg を上限として賃貸すること、使用済核燃料のアメリカへの返還、貸与燃料を目的どおり使用すること、使用記録を毎年報告することが取り決められたのである。

　その後改定を経て 1988 年 7 月に現行の、「原子力の平和的利用に関する協力のための日本国政府とアメリカ合衆国政府との間の協定（Agreement for Cooperation Between the Government of the United States of America and the Government of Japan Concerning Peaceful Uses of Nuclear Energy）」に至っている。協定はアメリカから日本への核燃料の調達だけでなく、再処理資機材・技術の導入などについても取り決めており、満期を迎える 2018 年 7 月の 6 か月前から文書で協定終了が通告されない限り、その効力は継続する。したがって日本が独自に原子力利用（あるいは利用しないこと）の方針を決めることは実質上困難な状態にあるが、そのことはあまり報じられていない。*The Atomic States of America* は福島の事故を踏まえたうえで、われわれも知るべき合衆国の「原子力平和利用」の実態をレポートしている。

Three Mile Island Nuclear Power Plant

The Atomic States of America (1)

Get Ready with Vocabulary

I 日本語に相当する英語を選びなさい。

1. 親戚	2. 葬式	3. 白血病	4. 施設	5. 災害
_____	_____	_____	_____	_____

6. 平和主義者	7. 亡命者	8. 残虐行為	9. 抵抗	10. 収入
_____	_____	_____	_____	_____

leukemia   relative   resistance   funeral   facility
pacifist   refugee   atrocity   income   disaster

II 日本語に相当するよう、選択肢を使って英語を完成しなさい。

radiation   generate   construction   power   reactor

1. 原子炉　　　　　　　**nuclear** [　　　　　　　　　]
2. 原子力発電所　　　　**nuclear** [　　　　　　　　　] **plant**
3. 放射能の毒性被害　　[　　　　　　　　] **poisoning**
4. 発電する　　　　　　[　　　　　　　] **electricity**
5. 工事中　　　　　　　**under** [　　　　　　　　]

34

Reading

America, the Atomic State

When Kelley McMasters grew up on Long Island, she took it for granted that almost every family had at least one cancer victim. The dying of friends, relatives and neighbors was so normal for her that she was shocked when, at her university in another town, people asked her why she went back home so often to attend funerals. It was then that it struck her that something was wrong with her hometown. This experience led her to write *Welcome to Shirley: Memoirs from an Atomic Town*, on which Don Argott and Sheena Joyce based their movie *The Atomic States of America* (2012).

McMasters' research revealed that her hometown Shirley in Long Island, and hundreds like it across the United States, were suffering from incredibly high cancer and leukemia rates. All these towns have either nuclear reactors or nuclear research laboratories, and most of the facilities were leaking and spilling contaminated substances that were poisoning and killing thousands of citizens.

The United States has the greatest number of nuclear power plants in the world: 104 to be exact, as of 2010, producing 20% of its energy. It is followed by France with 58 reactors, which produce 90% of its energy, and until the 2011 disaster, Japan with 54 producing 30%. The U.S., however, also has 60 national laboratories with their own nuclear reactors and 19 nuclear defense plants, making it by far the most dangerous country for radiation poisoning in the world.

Born Out of War

Nuclear power developed out of America's Manhattan project, which started in the Second World War at the behest of the Nobel laureate Albert Einstein*. Although a pacifist, as a Jewish refugee aware of the atrocities of the Nazis, Einstein

cancer victim 「癌で死亡した人」

it struck her ~ 「～と彼女は思いあたった」

contaminated substances 「汚染物質」

nuclear defense plants 「核防衛関連施設」

Manhattan project → Appendix 参照
at the behest of ~ 「～の要請を受けて」

35

feared that Germany was close to getting a nuclear bomb and felt the U.S.A. must get the bomb first to defeat it.

Top scientists from around the world developed the bombs that were soon to be tested on Hiroshima and Nagasaki. The U.S. believed the bombs would put a quick end to the war that was already costing millions of lives. As the Japanese fought so fiercely for the Pacific islands, the Americans feared the Japanese would put up an even stronger resistance on their homeland. But there is good argument that the bombs were dropped for other reasons, one being simply to test their unprecedentedly enormous destructive power. Some suggest that racist revenge was also a motive. Most certainly, it was also believed that demonstration of the bomb's power would stop the expansion in East Asia of the Soviet Union, which the U.S.A. already regarded as the major potential enemy of the post-war era.

After the war, the scientists, not wanting to lose funds and valuable research related to the atomic bombs, sought ways to use nuclear power for peaceful means. From food preservation with radioactive substances to blowing up cliffs with nuclear bombs to build dams, splitting atoms to generate electricity seemed the least crazy idea at the time.

At first, nuclear power seemed totally "green." "Clean, quiet and cheap," it looked like the savior of the modern world, because it could "meet ever-increasing energy demands without emitting exhaust and could limit dependence on other countries for energy." This same argument was used to sell nuclear power plants to Japan in the 1960s and 1970s, and is being used now both in Japan and the U.S. to encourage a nuclear renaissance.

Just One Bad Day

Then on March 28th, 1979, the Three Mile Island (TMI) nuclear reactor in Pennsylvania had a meltdown. While the power company announced, "Everything is under control,"

---

fiercely 「激しく」

unprecedentedly 「前代未聞の」

the post-war era 「第二次大戦後」しばしば米ソ冷戦期を指す

savior 「救世主」

exhaust 「排気ガス」ここでは主に CO_2 のこと

meltdown 「炉心溶融」

the public learned for the first time how they had been lied to, and how they had wrongly trusted their government and the power companies to ensure their safety.

At this point the government had plans to build a total of 250 nuclear power plants, only 110 of which were finished. But with the TMI meltdown, all power plants under construction or yet to be built were stopped due to public pressure. Or, if we believe the words of Arnold Gundersen, a former nuclear industry executive, construction stopped due to costs. In the 1970s, a nuclear power plant cost $3 to 4 billion to build, a coal plant only $400 million. Today the average cost of bringing a reactor online is $7 billion.

But the real costs of nuclear power were discovered later, only gradually. The TMI plant had run only 90 days when the meltdown occurred. It took until 1990 and over $1 billion to defuel it. Another $836.9 million is estimated as necessary to decommission and decontaminate the site. Note no medical costs are included in this figure. *The Wall Street Journal* reported in a 1991 study that the clean-up costs of the Chernobyl nuclear meltdown* were more than the income of all the other 54 reactors in the Soviet Union combined. As the film says, with nuclear power, one bad day wipes out decades of good days.

The Remains of the Chernobyl Nuclear Power Plant after the Meltdown

The Atomic States of America (1)

Albert Einstein 「アルバート・アインシュタイン」(1879-1955)

　　ドイツ生まれのアメリカ人物理学者。「相対性理論」で知られる。心の友ラテナウ（ワイマール共和国のユダヤ系外相）が暗殺され、自分の首にも懸賞金がかかっていた 1922 年、アインシュタインは日本を訪問し、43 日間の滞在中多くの知識人と意見を交わした。しかし日本への原爆投下については、『アインシュタイン平和書簡 3』（ネーサン、ノーデン編、金子敏男訳　みすず書房 1977 年）にわずかに言及があるだけである。「攻撃兵器の信じ難い発展の結果生まれた危険が、責任ある人々の本質的な変革をもたらしてもよかろうと、考えてもよいかに思われました。しかしこのような希望はあてにならぬことが証明されたのです」。(P.680) 原爆が実際に使えるようになってもそれを実際に使うことは起こりえないと信じていた、ということか。

the Chernobyl nuclear meltdown 「チェルノブイリ原発事故」

　　1986 年 4 月 26 日、ウクライナ（旧ソ連）のチェルノブイリ原子力発電所 4 号機で発生した原子炉事故。原子炉（黒鉛減速沸騰軽水圧力管型原子炉）の設計上の欠陥と操作ミスによって、動作試験中に反応度事故が発生。炉心溶融に続いて水蒸気爆発が起こり、原子炉や原子炉建屋が破壊され、大量の放射性物質が国境を越えて拡散した。爆発や急性放射線障害などで 31 人が死亡、11 万 6000 人が避難を強いられ、周辺地域の 6000 人以上の小児が甲状腺癌と診断されて 15 人が死亡している。国際原子力事象評価尺度で最も深刻なレベル 7 の事故に分類される。しかし 4 号炉は放射性物質の拡散を防止するための応急措置としてコンクリートの建造物（石棺）で覆われており、同発電所では事故後も他の原子炉が稼働し続け、2002 年 7 月にようやく閉鎖された。

以下の質問に日本語で答えなさい。

1. マックマスターズが自らの経験をきっかけとする調査で明らかにしたこととは何か。

2. アメリカは、戦後に向けたどのような戦略のために日本に原爆を投下したと推察できるか。

3. 1960 年代、1970 年代の日本、および近年アメリカの原子力ルネサンス推進において、原子力はどんな議論によって推奨されたか。

4. 250 ヵ所予定されていた原子力発電所の建設は TMI メルトダウンのあと中断された。アーニー・ガンダーソンによれば、その本当の理由は何か。

5. 『ウォール・ストリート・ジャーナル』によれば、チェルノブイリ事故の処理コストはどのようなものだったか。

38

Unit 7
The Atomic States of America <2>

President Jimmy Carter's Motorcade
Leaves Three Mile Island

President Carter Inspects the TMI Control Room
after the Accident

Anti-Nuclear Protestors at Washington D.C.

39

The Atomic States of America (2)

Get Ready with Vocabulary

Ⅰ　日本語に相当する英語を選びなさい。

1. 漏水　　　　**2.** 代表　　　　**3.** 偏った　　　　**4.** 告発者　　　　**5.** 上院議員

_____　　_____　　_____　　_____　　_____

6. 給与　　　　**7.** 猶予期間　　**8.** 原子力産業　**9.** 保証する　　**10.** 副大統領

_____　　_____　　_____　　_____　　_____

guarantee　　spill　　　　　　　whistleblower　　senator　　payroll
moratorium　　nuclear industry　representative　　biased　　vice-president

Ⅱ　日本語に相当するよう、選択肢を使って英語を完成しなさい。

extension　　expense　　denied　　outdated　　supervising

1. 監督庁　　　　　　　　　　　　　[　　　　　　　　] **agency**
2. 旧式の（耐用期間の過ぎた）発電所　[　　　　　　　　] **plant**
3. 営業許可延長　　　　　　　　　　**license** [　　　　　　]
4. 「営業許可 (延長) 却下」　　　　　**"license** [　　　　　　]**"**
5. まとまった出費　　　　　　　　　**capital** [　　　　　　]

40

Reading

The Failure of Consumer Protection

Watching *The Atomic States of America*, you may recall the frustration felt towards the Nuclear Regulation Authority of Japan* when listening to its explanations after
5 the Fukushima disaster. Can we trust our government and energy companies? The Nuclear Regulatory Commission (the NRC)*, the U.S. supervising agency which is supposed to protect the people from poorly run and outdated plants, has instead protected the nuclear power industry from
10 public knowledge and criticism. This is one of the key issues presented by this movie. The Commission members basically have given a green light to everything from spills to relicensing.

The list of leaks, spills and broken rules at plants all
15 around the country is long. In some towns, there are streets in which every single house has cancer victims. In Braidwood, Illinois, for example, one such "cancer-street" happens to run along the out-spill pipe of the local nuclear power plant. Radioactive cells of strontium-90, cesium-137*, iodine-131,
20 plutonium-239 and tritium have been found in the drinking water in this community. So, the residents of Braidwood must buy bottled water for drinking and cooking, despite the plentiful lakes and rivers they have in the area. The movie shows a scene of a Braidwood community meeting in which
25 representatives from the power company Exelon drink only bottled water while they claim that the water there is safe.

The NRC not only knew of the spills, they permitted them. Furthermore, to make up the reports on the Braidwood facility, the NRC used the private company's own, obviously
30 biased reports.

give a green light 「許可する」

radioactive 「放射性の」

Exelon 「エクセロン社」米大手電力・ガス会社。スリーマイルとブレイズウッドを含む 10 以上の電子力発電所を所有

41

Cost Above Safety: How Dangerous Aging Reactors Survive

Many of the nuclear reactors in America are now over 40 years old. In some plants, the condition of the machinery is appalling. Yet when such plants come up for review to renew their license for another 20 years, they are immediately accepted. Not a single nuclear power plant has been refused the license extension, not even the Vermont Yankee Plant whose water-cooling tower collapsed.

Paul Gallay, President of Riverkeeper, a group working to protect the Hudson River and the drinking water supplies for nine million New Yorkers, says, "I do not think they have a stamp in their office for 'License Denied'." Robert Alvarez, former senior policy advisor for the US Department of Energy, confesses that "the Nuclear Regulatory Commission is under a lot of pressure not to push for safety upgrades or require additional capital expenses."

As is typical with most giant American industries, power companies buy lobbyists who "persuade" congress to pressure the agencies set up to protect the consumer. One such example is the time when the NRC ordered the shutting down of the Millstone 1 nuclear power plant after a whistleblower made it public that the plant was "engaged in a very dangerous practice of pulling out its spent fuel before it should," in order to get new rods in more quickly to increase production. The company complained to Republican senator Pete Domenici of New Mexico*, who led the effort to put forward legislation which cut 700 NRC inspectors from the NRC payroll.

The Nuclear Renaissance*

Since the TMI meltdown*, a 30-year moratorium on nuclear power plants has existed in the States. However, since 9/11 and various terrorist threats, pressure has risen to develop energy sources at home. The nuclear industry has

---

appalling 「ぞっとするような」

the Vermont Yankee Plant 「バーモント・ヤンキー原発」1972 年から稼働。現在は廃炉作業中で 2075 年に終了予定

the US Department of Energy 「米エネルギー省」

the agencies set up to protect the consumer 消費者保護のための関係諸庁

rod 「核燃料棒」

taken this as an opportunity to start a Nuclear Renaissance, encouraging the building of new plants in America. In February 2010, President Obama guaranteed $8 Billion worth of loans to build a new nuclear power plant, the first in three decades, declaring, "The nation that leads clean energy, leads the global economy." Even the former vice-president Al Gore*, the author of *An Inconvenient Truth: The Planetary Emergency of Global Warming and What We Can Do about It* (2006), which warned about the coming global environmental crisis, was recommending nuclear power as a clean energy at this point.

An Inconvenient Truth
『不都合な真実』

Clean Up at Three Mile Island

The Atomic States of America (2)

the Nuclear Regulation Authority of Japan 「日本原子力規制委員会」

　　原子力規制委員会設置法に基づき設置された環境省の外局。委員会の事務局は原子力規制庁。国家行政組織法 3 条 2 項に基づいて設置される三条委員会と呼ばれる行政委員会で、法的には内閣からの独立性を保証される。「国民の生命、健康及び財産の保護、環境の保全並びに我が国の安全保障に資するため、原子力利用における安全の確保を図ること（原子力にかかる製錬、加工、貯蔵、再処理及び廃棄の事業並びに原子炉に関する規制に関すること、並びに国際約束に基づく保障措置の実施のための規制、その他の原子力の平和的利用の確保のための規制に関することを含む）を任務とする」と規定されている。

the Nuclear Regulatory Commission (the NRC) 「原子力規制委員会」

　　合衆国政府の独立機関の一つ。国内の原子力安全に関する監督業務を担当。原子炉の安全と、原子炉設置・運転免許の許認可と変更、放射性物質の安全と使用済み核燃料の管理 (貯蔵、保全、再処理と廃棄) を監督することになっている。

strontium-90, cesium-137 「ストロンチウム 90」「セシウム 137」

　　これらは福島原発事故のあと問題となっている物質でもある。

　　ストロンチウムという放射性物質は、セシウムと比べると揮発性が少なく、大気中に飛び出してきた量ということで比べると 1,000 分の 1 ぐらいで済むと推定できる。セシウムと同様、ストロンチウムも水に溶けやすく、溶け落ちた炉心に水をかけて冷やそうとすると放射能汚染水になる。セシウムは一部の粘土鉱物に非常に吸着しやすいという性質を持っており、たとえば東京電力はゼオライトという粘土鉱物を通すことによってセシウムを汚染水のなかから捕捉している。しかしストロンチウムは捕捉できず大量に含んだ水が海に流されている。一方セシウムはアルカリ金属元素類という元素類に属しており、同じくアルカリ金属元素に属するカリウムのように全身の筋肉組織に分布してゆく。したがって人がセシウムを摂取すると全身をくまなく被ばくさせることになる。一方ストロンチウムはアルカリ土類金属に属し、その中のカルシウムと同じく骨に蓄積する性質を持ち、摂取されると骨に溜まる。ストロンチウムに汚れた海で生きている魚も、中心的に溜まっている骨を食べずに身だけ食べるとすれば、ストロンチウム被ばくはかなり減らすことができる。（小出裕章、京都大学原子炉実験所助教、京都大学大学院工学研究科都市環境工学専攻助教　談）

Pete Domenici of New Mexico 「ニューメキシコ州選出のピート・ドメニチ」

　　本名ピエトロ・ヴィッキ・ドメニチ (1932-)。共和党。上院議員を 1973 年から 2009 年まで 6 期務めた。これはアメリカ最長。鉄道業界の要望を受けて水路使用料徴収を進め、電力業界の要請で原子力発電を進めた。

Nuclear Renaissance 「原子力ルネサンス」

　　2007 年から 2009 年、米原子力委員会に 13 の会社が 30 基の原子炉を国内に建設する申請を出した原子力拡大の動きを指す。その後、天然ガスの供給増や福島の事故を受けて、多くの申請が取りやめられた。それでも 2020 年までに、「福島」以前に契約がなっていた数基が建設される予定だが、一方で 2013-14 年には、カリフォルニア州サン・オノフレ 2 号機 3 号機、フロリダ州のクリスタル・リヴァー 3、ウィスコンシン州のキウォーニー、ヴァーモント州のヴァーモント・ヤンキーが閉鎖された。

TMI (Three Mile Island) Meltdown 「スリーマイル島炉心溶融事故」

　　スリーマイル島原子力発電所事故は、1979 年 3 月 28 日、97% の出力で運転中だった午前 4 時 37 分（現地時間）から起こった。脱塩塔（良好な処理水質を得るための装置）のイオン交換樹脂を再生するため

44

樹脂を移送作業中、樹脂が移送管に詰まり、樹脂移送用の水が弁などを制御する空気系に混入。異常を検知した脱塩塔出入口の弁が閉じ、主給水ポンプが停止。同時にタービンが停止した。二次冷却水の給水ポンプも止まったため蒸気発生器への冷却水の供給が行われず、一次冷却系を含む炉心の圧力が上昇して「加圧器逃し安全弁」が開いた。しかし圧力が下がっても弁は開いたまま固着して、大量の原子炉冷却材が蒸気となって失われた。原子炉では自動的に非常用炉心冷却装置が作動したが、すでに原子炉内の圧力が低下していて沸騰した冷却水が蒸気泡となって水位計に流入。そのため加圧器水位計は正しい水位を示さなかったので、運転員が冷却水過剰と誤った判断をし、非常用炉心冷却装置を手動で停止してしまう。そして一次系の給水ポンプも停止されたため、結局2時間20分開いたままになっていた安全弁から500トンの冷却水が流出し、炉心上部3分の2が蒸気中にむき出しとなり、熱によって燃料棒が破損した。運転員による給水回復措置が取られて事故が終息したときには、燃料の45%、62トンが溶融し、うち20トンが原子炉圧力容器の底に溜まっていた。

Al Gore 「アル・ゴア」Albert Arnold "Al" Gore, Jr.（1948- ）
　下院議員、上院議員、ビル・クリントン政権の副大統領。アメリカの政治家。地球温暖化の問題について警鐘を鳴らした映画『不都合な真実』の制作・出演者。2000年に大統領選挙では共和党候補ブッシュより得票数で上回ったが、フロリダ州での問題ある開票手続きのため落選が決定した。ゴアの情報スーパーハイウェイ構想に刺激されて世界にインターネットが爆発的に普及したことは有名である。ナノテクノロジーの研究に対して逸早く資金援助し、これも世界的に注目されるきっかけを作った。

以下の質問に日本語で答えなさい。

1. 米原子力規制委員会の犯した過ちとはどのようなものか。

2. イリノイ州ブレイズウッドでは、原子力発電所に関わるどんな問題が発生していたか。

3. 原子力規制委員会が営業停止を命じたマイルストーン1原子力発電所では、発電量を上げるためにどんなことが行われていたか。

4. 営業停止の勧告に対して電力会社はどう行動したか。

5. TMIメルドダウンから30年後、2010年、原子力発電をめぐってアメリカでどんな動きがあったか。

Unit 8
The Atomic States of America <3>

After the Explosion at Fukushima I

Anti-Nuclear Rally in September 2011 at Yoyogi Park

Get Ready with Vocabulary

I 日本語に相当する英語を選びなさい。

1. 勢い   2. 分離   3. 威嚇   4. 予知不可能であること   5. 海抜

_____   _____   _____   _____   _____

6. 退避   7. 土   8. 代替え   9. 愛着   10. 報償

_____   _____   _____   _____   _____

threat   attachment   above-sea-level   evacuation   momentum
breakaway   soil   alternative   remuneration   unpredictability

II 日本語に相当するよう、選択肢を使って英語を完成しなさい。

septic   radioactive   thermal   contingency   fault

1. 断層線   [   ] line
2. 偶発時への対応計画   [   ] plan
3. 放射能ゴミ   [   ] waste
4. 汚水浄化システム、汚水処理タンク装置   [   ] system
5. 火力発電（電力）   [   ] power

Indian Point Nuclear Power Plant

The Atomic states of America (3)

Reading

Lessons from Fukushima?

Despite countless problems with existing plants and fears of terrorist attacks, even the 3/11 disaster at Fukushima did not immediately stop the momentum to build new plants in the United States. In 2013, however, Obama finally suggested a possible breakaway from nuclear power, or at least a slowdown. Was he just taking the rise of shale gas into account? Or, after watching the coverage of the Fukushima disaster in Japan, did he consider how major accidents at nuclear power plants remain a huge threat to a nation and its people for an unpredictably long time?

Japanese power plants were designed by the same company that built most American plants: General Electric*. Many of them are aging and facing the same dangers as those in America. The Fukushima disaster has shown us that the plants are far from being safe or run competently. They were built against the will of many local people, who took the government to court to prevent construction, but lost. The court assured them of the safety of the plants. But the plants were placed at sea level to save money on the water

shale gas 「シェール・ガス」頁岩（けつがん）層から産出する天然ガス

took the government to court 「政府を訴えた」

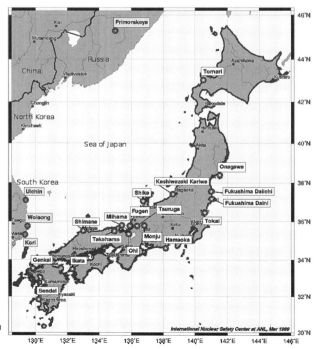

Map of Nuclear Power Plants in Japan

48

cooling system, not on a 15 meter rise as some experts had recommended, which may have saved the plants from the 2011 tsunami. It is also possible the backup-systems were faulty from the beginning.

25 The Fukushima disaster, with its 80km evacuation plan, woke up New Yorkers to the fact that the Indian Point nuclear power plant, one of the oldest plants in America, is only 55 km from Times Square. Then it was found that the plant is built just 1.5 km from two fault lines, on the most dangerous

30 potential earthquake spot in the U.S. The power company had no contingency plan for evacuating people beyond 16 km. With an 80 km evacuation plan applied, 20 million Americans would have to escape quickly. Would that be possible?

the Indian Point nuclear power plant 「インディアン・ポイント原子力発電所」二つの原子炉が 2013 年 と 2015 年 に 40 年の操業許可期間を終えたが、20 年の延長が許された

Waste and Dangers Stay

35 There have been at least 56 nuclear accidents in the United States since Chernobyl in 1986. Even without these accidents, the question of how to deal with radioactive waste remains unsolved for both "safely" working and post nuclear accident plants.

unsolved 「未解決の」

40 Japan has yet to come up with a solution to deal with the ever-increasing radioactive waste from Fukushima. Much of it is kept on the sight in large hastily built containers or buried in the ground, where it is most probably contaminating the ground water. Much of the contaminated soil has been

45 just gathered and covered with plastic sheets. Not a day has passed without hearing of a facility failure or worker injury, and the information we receive is just a part of what is going on. The costs of cleaning up Fukushima are horrendous, and the costs in lives, sickness, and lost houses and businesses are

horrendous 「恐ろしい」

50 really uncountable.

Eric Epstein is Chairman of Three Mile Island Alert*, an NPO which has been dedicated to the promotion of safe-energy alternatives since 1977, two years before the TMI meltdown. He points out, "We are not, as a species, mature enough to split the atom. There is too big an intersection between money and power that overrides safety." According to him, a nuclear power plant is "a toilet with no septic system." Each of the 100 plants in the U.S. produces one trainload of waste every 24 hours. That means millions of tons of waste over 30 years. "Though we must get rid of our dependency on oil to fight global warming, nuclear power is clearly not the solution."

The Fukushima disaster led Germany to the decision to shut down all of its nuclear power plants by 2022. The disaster also led to a 95% rejection of building new plants in Italy. In Sweden, where 40% of its electricity was nuclear, the new administration elected in September 2014 decided to abandon nuclear power generation.

The Decision of the Abe Administration

Yet the Abe administration retains its attachment to the old argument of nuclear energy being clean, and is about to reactivate some of the aging reactors. As of April 2015, the administration plans to restore over 20% of nuclear power by 2030. 25% of Japan's energy needs will be attained through renewable energies such as solar and wind. Thermal power, it is hoped, will generate the rest. Is this a good energy plan?

Under governmental protection, Japanese power companies have raised the electricity charges in stages and inconspicuously. They argue it is "because of the high costs of solar as well as thermal power generation. This excuse makes us suspect that they are trying to deter the promotion of renewable energies in order to hold onto nuclear power. Despite these claims of higher costs, the total amount of remuneration for the 22 directors of TEPCO in 2012 was over 0.23 billion yen. Since some of the directors had quit after the disaster, the amount per director was already 20 % higher from the previous year!

The Atomic States of America makes us rethink our choice

intersection between money and power 「金とパワーの交わるところ」("power" 電力と権力をかけている)

inconspicuously 「目立たぬように」

TEPCO 「東京電力」Tokyo Electric Power Company

UNIT 8

of energy production in the light of the track records of
90 nuclear plants in the U.S., and especially in the wake of the
Fukushima meltdown.

in the wake of 「～ に 注
目しながら」

General Electric　「ジェネラル・エレクトリック」（しばしば GE と表記）

　　世界最大の複合企業体。本社はコネチカット州。トマス・エディソンが 1878 年に始めたエジソン電気照明会社を吸収して 1889 年に設立されたエジソン総合電気 Edison General Electric Company が始まり。ダウ平均株価の構成銘柄のうち、1896 年 5 月 26 日の算出開始以来唯一残っている企業。

　　ジャック・ウェルチ CEO（1981-2001）以降、ますます世界規模の柔軟な事業展開を続け、デルタ航空を買収、世界シェアで 3 位以下になった電機部門を中国ハイアールに売却、2014 年には家電部門すべてをエレクトロラックス（スウェーデンの世界最大の家電メーカー）に売却など動きが激しい。1964 年には東芝とコンピューター技術の提携、1971 年には三井化学、長瀬産業と 3 社合弁の日本 GE プラスティックス社を設立（2007 年に発展的解消）。1990 年代には傘下の GE キャピタルの子会社ゲートファイナンス株式会社が、日本の機械メーカーミネベアからミネベア信販を買収。NC カード仙台のクレジットカード事業も取得し、日本の信販事業に参入。1998 年には東邦生命保険と共同出資でエジソン生命保険を設立（その後 AIG に売却）、同年、幸福銀行子会社を買収して日本の消費者金融に進出。2000 年代に入ってからは三洋電機クレジットの買収、GE ヘルスケアジャパン設立など、日本経済との関わりも深く長い。2010 年、日本 GE と GE フィナンシャルサービスが合併し、日本ではしばらく金融色が目立っていた。しかし 2006 年には日立製作所と GE 双方の原子力部門を統合し、日立 GE ニュークリア・エナジーが設立されている。

Three Mile Island Alert　「スリーマイル島アラート」

　　原子力に変わる安全な代替えエネルギーの普及促進を目的とする NPO。TMI メルトダウンの 2 年前の 1977 年設立。スリーマイル島のあるペンシルバニアに拠点を置き、放射能のモニタリング、低レベル放射性ゴミの管理、スリーマイル島原発による健康被害、原発の安全管理の監視といった問題に取り組んでいる。

以下の質問に日本語で答えなさい。

1. 2013 年、オバマ大統領が原子力推進に慎重になった要因と推測できるできごとを 2 点挙げよ。

2. 福島の事故後、インディアン・ポイント原子力発電所についてどんなことが新たにわかったか。

3. エリック・エプスタインに原子力発電を何に例えているか。それはなぜか。

4. 日本の電力会社は、何を電気料金値上げの理由としているか。

5. 福島の事故の翌年、東京電力の役員報酬は前年に比べてどうだったか。

51

Who Killed the Electric Car? <1>

　最近のアメリカは石油大国でありながら「脱石油依存」を目指すオバマ政権のもと、電気自動車開発に邁進している。映画 ***Revenge of the Electric Car*** 『電気自動車の逆襲』（2011、劇場は未公開）は、宇宙船打ち上げを行うスペース X 社などを創業した米ベンチャー界の革命児、イーロン・マスクを主役とし、彼の電気自動車会社テスラ社と米ゼネラルモーターズ、そしてカルロス・ゴーン社長率いる日産自動車の 3 社を軸に白熱する電気自動車開発競争を取材している。実はその映画の監督クリス・ペインは 2006 年封切りの『誰が電気自動車を殺したか』で、ブッシュ政権下、電気自動車がいかにして抹殺されたかを暴いていた。

　この映画は、ゼネラルモーターズが 1996 年にリース発売した電気自動車「EV1」を中心に展開する。カリフォルニア州の排ガス規制にも対応できる夢の車 EV1。一部の利用者に熱狂的に支持されたが、自動車業界そのものや石油会社から訴訟などの反撃を受け、業界と癒着するブッシュ政権が州政府に圧力をかけた。排ガス規制を進めていた州当局はこれに屈し、規制は弱められた。自動車業界も利益率の低い電気自動車への意欲を失い、GM は「需要がない」と車の強制回収を決めた。後に、充電設備に税金をつぎ込むことに反対した消費者団体の背後に石油業界がいたことが判明している。2003 年、利用者たちの抵抗むなしく EV1 は回収され、スクラップの山と化す。映画はそうした経緯描き、数々の賞を受賞し、世界の自動車業界に衝撃を与えた。

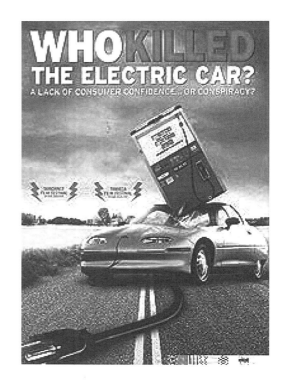

UNIT 9

Get Ready with Vocabulary

I 日本語に相当する英語を選びなさい。

1. 大惨事	2. 車体	3. 繁栄する	4. 喘息	5. 排気ガス
_____	_____	_____	_____	_____

6. 喪に服す	7. 容疑者	8. 有罪である	9. 犯人	10. 株
_____	_____	_____	_____	_____

guilty　　culprit　　mourn　　suspect　　share
vehicle　　flourish　　catastrophe　　asthma　　exhaust

II 日本語に相当するよう、選択肢を使って英語を完成しなさい。

East　　conscious　　federal　　pollution　　mandate

1. 大気汚染　　　　　air ［　　　　　　　　］
2. 中東　　　　　　　the Middle ［　　　　　　　］
3. 低排出量命令　　　zero emission ［　　　　　　　］
4. 連邦政府　　　　　the ［　　　　　　　　］ government
5. 環境意識のある　　environmentally ［　　　　　　　］

53

Reading

A Funeral

Most of the troubles in our world today begin with cars and oil: air pollution, lung sicknesses, global warming and the related catastrophes, as well as the wars in the Middle East and ensuing terrors. But what if we could invent a car that used no oil and did not pollute? What if we had a decent electric car, for example? Would that not solve most of our problems?

As a matter of fact, General Motors (GM)* already invented such a car, and it was produced and sold in California in the 1990s. Then, why do so few people know about it? Why do we no longer see it on the road? These questions are all answered by the documentary film, *Who Killed the Electric Car?* (2006)

This film begins at a funeral that took place on July 24th, 2003 at the Hollywood Forever Cemetery, in Los Angeles, California. We see people dressed in black among gravestones as a man gives a eulogy. It is not a funeral for a person. It is a funeral for a car called the EV1, designed and produced by GM around 1990. EV stands for "electric vehicle." This funeral marked the end of a battle for the future. The future with peaceful electric cars and clean air lost to gas cars and pollution.

ensuing 「続く」
decent 「まともな」

eulogy 「賛辞」

Thomas Parker Electric Car 1880s

Thomas Edison Electric Car 1913

This was not the first such war lost. The very first cars in the late 19th and early 20th centuries were electric. They were popular because they were quiet, did not smell nor require cranking to start. But then in the 1920s, the automatic starter was invented, gas cars were mass-produced, and cheaper gas became available because of newly discovered oil fields in America and western control of Middle East oil producing regions as a result of World War I. In consequence, electric cars were pushed off the market by the growing power of car companies.

cranking 「クランク回し」

Electric Cars Flourished and Disappeared Again

However, by 1990 two things had happened that would bring back the electric car. First, in 1973, the Organization of the Petroleum Exporting Countries (OPEC)*, mainly made up of the Middle East oil producing nations, put an oil embargo on the U.S.A. It was a response to American support of Israel in the Yom Kippur War. Oil shortages pushed up oil prices from $3.00 to $12.00 a gallon. This energy crisis gave America a need to develop alternative energies, a desire not to depend on foreign oil, and left a lasting effect on government policy.

the Yom Kippur War 「第四次中東戦争」ユダヤ暦の贖罪の日（ヨム・キプール）に始まった、中東とイスラエルの戦争

Secondly, air pollution reached all-time highs, especially in Los Angeles, an automobile city with the worst air pollution in the country. Children were often not allowed to

General Motor's 1990s Electric Vehicle, EV1

play outside because of the smog. About 25 % of all 15 to 25 year olds were found to have severe lung problems such as asthma and cancer. The California Air Resources Board (CARB)* introduced a zero emissions mandate in the 1990s: all new cars would have to reduce exhaust by 2% by 1998, 5% by 2001 and 10% by 2003, eventually leading to zero emissions.

Responding to this regulation, car companies started to experiment with their own designs. GM spent billions of dollars to produce the EV1, the first new electric car in almost a century. Hundreds of them were leased. The users loved them for they were fast, silent, chargeable at home, not so expensive and "sexy." Hollywood stars like Tom Hanks and Mel Gibson bought them up and boasted how they were helping save America by not polluting as they drove.

But soon there were not enough EV1s. And not only were people on a waiting list, but GM started selecting buyers. Mel Gibson had to fill in a long resume with ridiculously personal details to see if he "merited" owning one. Other users were denied a renewal of their lease and had to resist the company to keep their cars. In the end, GM took back all the EVs and its EV1 sales teams were laid off. Honda, Toyota, Ford, and Nissan followed suit, recalling their EVs.

chargeable　「充電できる」

boast　「自慢する」

merit ~　「～に値する」

were laid off　「解雇された」
follow suit　「先例に従う」

Crushed EV1s

By 1996, there were EVs all over California. Ten years later they were all gone. The last GM EV1 was destroyed on March 14th, 2005. The companies had not only taken the cars off the road, but crushed them to remove all trace of their electric vehicles. Many EV users were left feeling like they had lost something they loved, and mourned as if a person, not a car, had died.

The Suspects

Who murdered the electric cars? The suspects investigated in this film are: consumers, batteries, oil companies, car companies, the US federal government, the CARB, and hydrogen fuel cells.

At first glance, consumers are found guilty for many would not consider buying an electric car, worrying that its distance limit of 60 miles per charge would spoil their freedom, even though 90% of people drive a maximum of 29 miles a day. However, in truth, there was a huge market for the cars in the environmentally conscious state of California and there were long waiting lists for the cars. As the EV1 sales people and drivers pointed out over and over, people were ready to embrace electric cars if they were properly marketed. But GM did not really promote the EVs. They did not produce the usual slick car commercials known to sell cars, nor answer the basic questions in prospective buyers' minds: how much, how far, how fast can the cars go. It was as if they did not want to sell the EV. It is a group of consumers that leads the battle to bring back the electric car. After all, consumers are not the major culprit.

How about batteries? They were accused of not being good enough for the cars to drive far enough for consumer likes. Actually however, a new battery that rendered electric cars no less efficient, and even cheaper to run than gas cars, had already been invented. It is this battery that is now loaded in the hybrid cars made by Toyota, Honda and other

embrace 「大歓迎する」
were properly marketed 「適切に市場に出される」「ちゃんと広告される」
slick 「巧みな」

culprit 「犯罪者」

57

companies. GM, instead of using this for their EVs, bought up the shares of the battery company and sold them to Chevron-Texaco*. This oil giant killed the batteries by refusing to sell them. The batteries are another victim, not a murderer.

General Motors 「ジェネラル・モーターズ」General Motors Company　（略称 GM）

　本社をミシガン州デトロイトにおく自動車メーカー。20 世紀初めからライバルのフォード社と競合してアメリカの自動車産業を支えてきたが、20 世紀末からの「脱オイル」と小型車人気に乗り遅れ、リーマンショック後の 2009 年 6 月 1 日に連邦倒産法第 11 章の適用を申請。2013 年 12 月 9 日にアメリカ合衆国財務省が保有する GM の株式を全て売却処分し国有化が終了。2013 年に女性 CEO 就任で話題となったが、破綻と再生の在り方は厳しく評価されている。

　長年 GM はデトロイト市の事実上の主であり、その再生のためオバマ大統領は 800 億ドルの税金投入を許し、巨額の法人税の支払いを免除した。しかし GM はその資金をデトロイト市でなく、販売台数の半分を占める新興国に投資。また、デトロイトの工場では新規労働者の賃金半減や 8 時間だった労働時間の上限撤廃、年金の大幅カット、不採算工場の閉鎖などをおこなった。黒字に転化した GM は経営破綻から 1 年 5 ヵ月という異例の早さで株式市場に再上場し、役員たちは数百万ドル（数億円）のボーナスを手にした。他方デトロイト市では労働者の賃金は大幅に下がり、大量に生まれたワーキングプア層が SNAP（低所得層への食料支援プログラム）受給者となるなど州や市の財政を圧迫。デトロイト市内の自動車関連の就業者はピーク時の 10 分の 1 に落ち込み、工場移転で失業率は 50％となり、市の税収は下がり続け借金を重ねたあげく、ついに歳入の 13 倍近い 180 億ドル（約 2 兆円）超という、米自治体として最大規模の負債で財政破綻した。負の部分はすべて行政や国家に転嫁し企業は利益だけを獲得するという、アメリカ資本主義の限界を象徴するできごとだと批判されている。血税で救済されながら、地域経済や雇用、住民生活に対する社会的責任を投げ出すという資本側の姿は、格差を生む社会構造への問題意識を高めた。

OPEC 「石油輸出国機構」

　加盟国はサウジアラビア、イラン、イラク、UAE、クウェート、カタール、アルジェリア、ナイジェリア、リビア、インドネシア、ベネズエラ、エクアドル、アンゴラ。産油国側の利益を守る目的で 1960 年、中東の産油国を中心として設立。石油生産量や価格の調整をするための役割を果たす。近年はロシアやメキシコの油田、北海油田といった、OPEC 以外の油田の生産量が増し、またシェールガスなど天然ガスを始めとする石油以外のエネルギー供給があるため、その影響力は相対的には低下した。しかし OPEC 加盟国の原油生産量は世界のおよそ半分近くを占め、世界のエネルギーバランスにおける比重は依然として大きい。近年さらにイラン産原油取引に対する制裁が段階的に解除される見通しがある。

the California Air Resources Board 「カリフォルニア空気資源委員会」

　1967 年発足の、カリフォルニア州政府環境保護庁所属の言わば「きれいな空気担当部」。政府外の科学者など専門家からなる。連邦政府の「クリーン・エア法」成立以前に独自の基準を決定。他の州が連邦政府の基準を採用するなか、独自の基準にそった低公害車（エコカー）普及を政策目的にかかげる。

Chevron-Texaco 「シェブロン・テキサコ」

　シェブロンはカリフォルニア州サンモランに本社を置く石油関連企業。石油などエネルギー関連製品を

扱う企業。現在世界の石油関連企業の中でも特に巨大な規模を持つ国際石油資本（スーパーメジャー）6社の一つである。1991年から2001年、ライス国務長官が取締役として在職していた。テキサコは1901年、テキサス州ボーモントで創立。1914年に本社をニューヨーク州ハリソンに移転。第二次大戦後から1970年代はメジャーの一つだったが2001年2月1日にシェブロンと統合、シェブロン・テキサコとなった。2005年に再び社名がシェブロンとなり、会社としてのテキサコは消滅し今はシェブロンの石油ブランドである。

以下の質問に日本語で答えなさい。

1. 1920年代、電気自動車はなぜ姿を消していったのか。

2. 1990年までに、電気自動車の再登場を促すどのようなことが起こっていたか。2点挙げよ。

3. カリフォルニア州の「自動車の排気ガスをゼロに近づける」条例は、カリフォルニアのカーライフに一時的にせよどのような変化を起こしたか。

4. その後、消費者が電気自動車の購入をためらったのはなぜか。

5. 電気自動車をガソリン車より費用効率の良い乗り物にする電池は、発明された後、どうなったのか。

Unit 10

Who Killed the Electric Car? <2>

Ides of the EV1

UNIT 10

Get Ready with Vocabulary

I 日本語に相当する英語を選びなさい。

1. 嘘の	**2.** 広告	**3.** 論説	**4.** に匹敵する	**5.** メンテナンス
_____	_____	_____	_____	_____

6. 支配する	**7.** 殲滅する	**8.** 宥める	**9.** 見積もる	**10.** ちらっと見せびらかす
_____	_____	_____	_____	_____

equal   estimate   flash   maintenance   dominate
false   editorial   advertisement   annihilate   appease

II 日本語に相当するよう、選択肢を使って英語を完成しなさい。

deduction   local   willing   pass   annual

1. 地方自治体   [   ] **government**
2. 年間利益   [   ] **profit**
3. 税控除   **tax** [   ]
4. 購買意欲のある客   [   ] **customer**
5. 亡くなる   [   ] **away**

61

Reading

The Main Culprits

The oil companies are guilty, for they actively campaigned against the electric car to ensure people continued to use gas cars. They started false consumer groups voicing against
5 EVs. They pressured both the federal and local governments not to set up electric recharge stations, arguing that it was an abuse of tax-payers' money. They released advertisements and editorials in newspapers to give false information, such as that electric cars pollute the air more than gas cars as they
10 use electricity from coal-generated power plants. Scientific studies showed otherwise. Also, together with car companies, they pressured CARB to scrap the emissions mandate. What was the oil companies' motivation? Greed. In 2003, the US oil industry was making $33 billion in annual profit. By 2005,
15 with the death of the EVs, it was making $64 billion.

The federal government, in particular the Bush administration, is also guilty. With more states such as New York, New Jersey, Maine and Vermont considering following California, the administration sued the state of California over
20 the mandate in order to stop the development of EVs. The

voice against「反対の声をあげる」

abuse of tax-payers' money「納税者の金の濫用」「税金の無駄使い」

coal-generated power plant「火力発電」
otherwise「そうではないと」
scrap ここでは「廃止する」

The GM Hummer: The Biggest Gas-Guzzling Car in the World

government used both stick and carrot to discourage EVs. In 2002, the largest tax deduction for an EV was $4,000. But in 2003, a $100,000 tax credit was given for buying a Hummer, the largest and most gas-guzzling car in the world. The amount almost equaled the entire price of the car!

The car companies are guilty too, for they could not figure out how electric cars would make them enough profit. They did not move to mass production and refused to sell or continue to lease electric cars to willing customers. They even funded the grassroots movement to repeal the CARB mandate and made advertisements that discouraged EV sales. Why? They had become afraid that if consumers welcomed EVs, all their regular models would soon stop selling. Besides, they feared to lose after-sale profits brought by oil filters, oil changes and starters. EV maintenance is easy and low cost. GM stopped producing the EV1 in 1999, one month after they started producing Hummers.

Oil Dominates and Deters

Why would the US government support gas cars against zero emission vehicles in this age of global warming? The answer involves its desire for world control. At the time the Bush administration tried to annihilate the electric cars, it was also involved in the war in Iraq. Now it is known that the U.S. Vice President Dick Cheney made an enormous profit through the war for his company Halliburton, which mainly explores oil and natural gas fields to build facilities for energy production. The oil and car companies also benefitted from control over Iraqi oil. Some in the administration were former car company CEOs, such as Andrew H. Card*. He was White House Chief of Staff under George Bush from 2001 to 2006, and head of Bush's White House Iraq Group. He previously served as United States Secretary of Transportation under President Bush Sr. from 1992 to 1993, and was vice president of the American Automobile Manufacturers Association.

Dick Cheney

In short, the car companies were extremely close to the government and had many ways to "bring governments to their knees," as consumer advocate Ralph Nader says in the movie.

The Bush administration also crushed a hybrid car research program that had been promoted to the car companies under the Clinton administration. In spite of the great advances in hybrid technology, they scrapped the program as soon as Bush allowed them to. The irony is that Toyota and Honda, fearing their companies would be left behind by the program, developed their own hybrids such as the Prius series. As a result, they now make huge profits in hybrid sales while Ford and GM, who were once ahead, lost out in the game.

Environmental Lip Service

As Wally E. Rippell, a research engineer for AeroVironment* in California, says, "The federal government is using our taxes to support car companies, and our military to get oil, instead of using it to prepare for a better future." Facing the overwhelming evidence of global warming presented by scientists, the federal government talks about the environment to appease the public now and then. But it is just lip service or "music for environmentalists," as pointed out by David Freeman, a former energy advisor for the Carter Administration.

One song the Bush administration sang was the funding of the hydrogen fuel cell car, which is supposed to be cleaner and safer than EVs. It sounded fabulous, but the reality is disappointing. First, the estimated cost per vehicle was over a million dollars, way beyond the consumers' wallet. Second, it is not easy to secure storage room for the fuel in the car. Besides, the hydrogen fuel is estimated to be two to three times more expensive than gasoline. Finally, those cars would require an infrastructure of at least 20,000 hydrogen stations. Now many suspect that the government flashed the hydrogen car as an environmentally friendly smokescreen, as it is near impossible to produce successfully.

In summary, the real culprit in the death of the electric car is a combination of the government, oil and car companies, who desire to ensure their excessive profits and control the energy supply in the world.

Grassroots Hope

Thankfully, there are new ways that will sidestep the car companies. The movie ends with a grassroots movement of citizens who are trying to bring back electric cars. Stanford R. Ovshinsky*, the inventor of the new battery, says in the movie that it is better to fight this battle for the future with better science than with guns. He set up a solar power factory making thin, cheap, easy-to-put-up solar panels.

Unlike hydrogen cars, electric cars can be charged at home without expensive infrastructure. Indeed they have been on the road and are ready for us now.

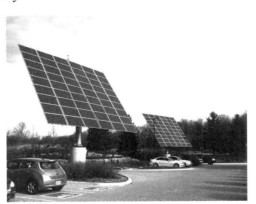

The Earth Rangers Solar Power Station

Andrew H. Card
　レーガン政権で政府間問題担当大統領特別補佐官を、ブッシュ（父）大統領のもとで運輸長官を、ブッシュ（子）大統領の首席補佐官を務めた。イラク侵攻の正当性を掲げ、戦争支持の世論形成の役割を担った。イラク戦争がもうひとつのベトナム戦争と見做されることを懸念してネオコンのラムズフェルド国防長官を退けるよう大統領の説得を試みて失敗した。このため 2006 年に辞任したとされる。GM の破たん処理にも関わり、特別補佐官辞任直後からユニオン・パシフィック鉄道の取締役。

AeroVironment 「エアロビロンメント」

　1971 年設立の、カリフォルニアを拠点とする車体技術開発会社。電気自動車や無人飛行機やドローンの開発で知られる。飛行物体監視機を開発中の兵器大手ロッキード・マーティン社と技術提携をし、国防省に Raven（鴉）、Wasp（蜂）、 Puma（ピューマ）といったドローンを供給する。

Stanford R. Ovshinsky（1922-2012）「スタンフォード・オブシンスキー」

　「現代のエジソン」と称されるアメリカ人発明家。父はリトアニアからの亡命ユダヤ人。 高校卒業後、大学へ進学せず図書館で独学し、24 歳で自動旋盤機の設計で特許を取得。その後会社を設立し、水素燃料、半導体、蓄電などの関連で新技術を次々生み出す。 それらは後に太陽光パネルや薄型テレビ、ハイブリッドカーに応用され、 環境分野での活躍から「惑星（地球）の英雄」と呼ぶ人もいる。大学の学位もなく発想が奇抜過ぎるとして、当初その発明は冷笑されたが、1970 年代、彼の才能に気付いた日本企業がアイデアを製品化していった。「日本企業が来てから米企業が私に関心を示した」と後に語っている。米国の平均的企業では社長の給与は一般社員の約 500 倍だがオブシンスキーの会社では 5 倍。 しかも経営者でありながら労働組合員だった。350 以上の特許を持ちながら、技術開発費を惜しまなかったため会社は損を出し続け、「利益だけは作れない発明家」「40 年間で 36 年も赤字を出して生き残る記録的会社」とメディアに書かれた。とうとう 2007 年 84 歳で、投資家の期待には背き続けることは不可能と判断した自分の会社に解雇されたが、「私の仕事は、平和と市民の権利と自由、そして労働者のためだった」とインタヴューに答えた。 （『毎日新聞』2012. 10. 31）

以下の質問に日本語で答えなさい。

1. 石油会社は電気自動車を潰すためにどんな手を使ったか。連邦政府の「飴と鞭」の政策とは何か。自動車会社はなぜ電気自動車から手を引いたのか。

2. 地球温暖化が危惧される時代にブッシュ政権はなぜ、環境に良い電気自動車を殲滅してガソリン車を擁護しようとしたのか。

3. ブッシュ政権がハイブリッド車を潰した結果、どんな皮肉なことが起こったか。

4. ブッシュ政権が推進するフリをした水素自動車とは、実際どのようなものか。その普及を阻む欠点を 3 点指摘せよ。

5. かつて電気自動車に使える新型電池を開発したスタンフォード・オブシンスキーは何を設立したか。

Unit 11

The Fog of War:

Eleven Lessons from the life of Robert S. McNamara <1>

　ロバート・マクナマラは第二次世界大戦中の1943年、勤務先であるハーヴァード大学と政府との提携によって軍に配属され、統計管理局で戦略爆撃の解析および立案の仕事に従事した。1945年にドイツの敗北が決定的になると、陸軍航空軍は余っていたB-17戦闘機を極東に転用して日本を爆撃しようとしたが、マクナマラら統計管理局の若手将校たちは、統計学を用いた分析で、新型大型爆撃機B-29を大量生産し対日戦に投入する方がコスト面で効率的であると主張。その意見は採用され、B-29を対日戦略爆撃に大量投入することで、大きな戦果を上げる。しかし日本諸都市への無差別爆撃に対する倫理性についてはかねてより上官だったカーティス・ルメイに帰しており、この映画でもそう主張している。戦後はフォード社の経営に携わり、大胆なリストラと不採算工場の閉鎖でコストを大幅に削減し経営効率を高め、社長となったあと、ケネディとジョンソン大統領の国務長官としてベトナム戦争に関わる。

　「日本への爆撃は、求める効果に対して規模が大きすぎた。」「ベトナム戦争は誤りだった。」この映画は、冷徹な手法で「人間計算機」とも評されたマクナマラが、未公開資料にも触れつつ30年近い沈黙を破ってカメラの前で語った生々しい証言であり、人間マクナマラを感じさせる世紀の告白である。アメリカではベトナム戦争をめぐる映画中の発言が注目された。

　日本爆撃を彼がどうふり返っているのか。われわれにとってはやはりそれがこの映画の一つの焦点だろう。彼は戦争犯罪人なのか。それ自体破壊と殺戮行為である戦争において「犯罪人」という概念はあるのか。誰がそれを決めるのか。疑問は残る。

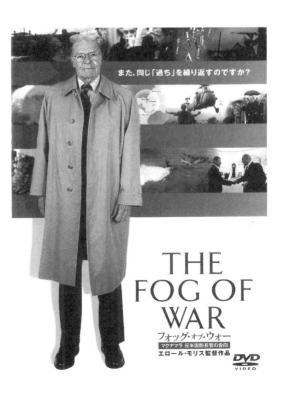

The Fog of War: Eleven Lessons from the Life of Robert S. McNamara (1)

Get Ready with Vocabulary

I 日本語に相当する英語を選びなさい。

1. 将軍	**2.** 記憶	**3.** 告白の	**4.** 共感する	**5.** 相反する
＿＿＿＿＿＿＿	＿＿＿＿＿＿＿	＿＿＿＿＿＿＿	＿＿＿＿＿＿＿	＿＿＿＿＿＿＿

6. 大使	**7.** 合理性	**8.** 候補	**9.** 民間人	**10.** 人口統計
＿＿＿＿＿＿＿	＿＿＿＿＿＿＿	＿＿＿＿＿＿＿	＿＿＿＿＿＿＿	＿＿＿＿＿＿＿

confessional　　empathize　　conflicting　　recollection　　ambassador
demographics　　rationality　　candidate　　civilian　　general

II 日本語に相当するよう、選択肢を使って英語を完成しなさい。

criminal　　missile　　disproportional　　budget　　efficiency

1. 効率性についての報告　　[　　　　　　　] **report**
2. 戦争犯罪人　　　　　　　**war** [　　　　　　　]
3. 核ミサイル　　　　　　　**nuclear** [　　　　　　　]
4. 不釣り合いな規模　　　　[　　　　　　　] **scale**
5. 防衛予算　　　　　　　　**defense** [　　　　　　　]

68

Reading

  The Vietnam War lasted almost 20 years from November 1st 1955 to April 30th 1975. It resulted in the deaths of 58,000 American soldiers and up to 3.5 million Vietnamese soldiers and citizens, in addition to over 200,000 deaths in Laos and Cambodia each. *The Fog of War* (2003) tells the story of the man widely held responsible for that war, Robert Strange McNamara (1916-2009).

  McNamara's decisions also greatly affected Japan. Not many Japanese know that an efficiency report made by him quite possibly led General Curtis LeMay to decide on firebombing 57 Japanese cities in the Second World War. The actions resulted in the deaths of 50% to 90% of their populations.

General Curtis LeMay → Appendix 参照

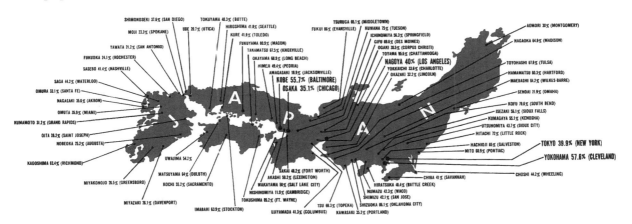

Map of Principle Japanese Cities Destroyed by Firebombing, with percentage of area destroyed and an equivalent U.S. city in brackets

＜上の図＞
B-29 の爆撃によって破壊された日本の主要都市。数字は破壊された割合を示す。同規模のアメリカの都市名が比較のために記されている

  The movie raises the question as to whether he is a war criminal. His main defense is that generals and politicians make mistakes in the fog of war, and that he himself always acted with the aim of saving as many lives as possible. His down-to-earth and conscientious character almost convinces us of his point of view.

  Errol Morris, the director of *The Fog of War*, interviewed McNamara for over twenty hours and edited his recollections. Along with historical footage and 11 self-drawn lessons from the experiences of this man, who is often regarded as a cost-performance war criminal, the movie leads us to rethink what the wars were and who is responsible for them.

Lesson 1 "Empathize with your enemy."

First, recounting the events of the Cuban Missile Crisis (October 14-28, 1962), McNamara illustrates how close America came to nuclear war. Though he and President Kennedy wanted to keep the nation out of war, some others within the White House were for invading Cuba. During this crisis, Kennedy received two conflicting messages from Nikita Khrushchev*, then General Secretary of the Communist Party of the Soviet Union. The "soft message" arrived first, ensuring that the Soviet Union will remove the nuclear missiles from Cuba if the U.S. promises not to invade. Before Kennedy could respond, however, the "hard message" came, declaring that, "the U.S.S.R.* will respond with massive amounts of force if the U.S. does invade Cuba."

It was the ambassador to Moscow, Llewellyn "Tommy" Thompson who, based on personal knowledge of Khrushchev and analysis of the situation, persuaded Kennedy not to take military action . He showed Kennedy that it was more important to Khrushchev to be able to tell his people that he saved communist Cuba from US invasion than to take the risk of war. Kennedy was convinced and decided against the invasion. According to McNamara, it was Thompson's ability to empathize with Khrushchev's viewpoint that prevented a nuclear war.

U.S. Helicopter Hovers Over Soviet B-59 Submarine on its Way to Cuba

U.S. Neptune Flies Over Soviet Ship Carrying Missiles to Cuba

Lessons 2 and 3 "Rationality alone will not save us," and "there's something beyond one's self."

McNamara, though often criticized as a cold, inhuman rationalist, argues against a purely rational leadership in this interview. He points out that rational individuals nearly chose nuclear war and that it was partly luck that avoided the Cuban missile crisis. He stresses that the potential for nuclear war still exists, and warns that, "While all military commanders make mistakes and try to learn from them, there will be no learning period with nuclear weapons. A single mistake will lead to a major catastrophe."

The movie covers events in his life that contributed to policy decisions he made later on as Defense Secretary. In particular, he was influenced by the logic and ethics of Plato and Aristotle whom he studied at U.C. Berkeley along with Economics and Mathematics. These philosophers gave him a strong sense of duty to the state, as well as the sense that there is something beyond one's self. After graduating from U.C. Berkeley he went on to the Harvard Graduate School of Business. McNamara was an assistant professor at Harvard when his country entered the Second World War. At that time the university had just accepted a contract with the government to start an officer candidate school for Statistical Control in the US Air Force.

Lessons 4 and 5 "Maximize efficiency," and "proportionality should be a guideline in war."

It was in this position at Harvard that McNamara came to work on statistical analysis as an officer, increasing the efficiency of bombing campaigns in Germany with General Curtis LeMay. McNamara followed LeMay into the Pacific theater and thus his reports on efficiency contributed to LeMay's decision to fly B29 bombers low and begin firebombing Japanese cities.

McNamara, however, poses the question: whether it was

---

inhuman rationalist 「非人間的合理主義者」

Defense Secretary 「国防長官」
Plato and Aristotle 「プラトンとアリストテレス」
U. C. Berkeley 「カリフォルニア州立大学バークレー校」

the Harvard Graduate School of Business 「ハーヴァード経営大学院」

officer 「士官」
statistical control 「統計的管理」

the Pacific theater 「太平洋戦区」

fly ~ low 「低空飛行させる」

necessary to drop two atomic bombs on Japan when so much had already been destroyed with firebombing. The Japanese cities destroyed in the firebombing are: Tokyo, roughly the size of New York at that time, 51% destroyed; Toyama, the size of Chattanooga, 99% destroyed; Nagoya, the size of Los Angeles, 40% destroyed; Osaka, the size of Chicago, 35% destroyed. The bombings killed 50% to 90% of people in each of these cities. More than 100,000 civilians died in Tokyo alone.

McNamara states in the movie that LeMay felt he had to destroy Japan, for he believed he would be considered a war criminal if America lost the war. Regardless of the various justifications given, McNamara now accepts that LeMay's actions, and quite possibly his own too, qualify as crimes against humanity. But McNamara does not wholly disavow the bombings. He only regrets their disproportional scale.

disavow 「否定する」

Lesson 6 "Get the Data."

After the war, McNamara began working for Ford Motor Company, which was falling behind GM and needed leadership from people with higher education. As an executive, he commissioned several studies aimed at getting information on statistics from buyer demographics for certain vehicles to accident reports to make cars safer. He used this data to design cars which brought the company great successes.

commission 「委託する」「依頼する」

The Firebombing of Tokyo,
View from U.S. Bomber

The Remains of Nagasaki
after the Nuclear Bomb

UNIT 11

110　　　In July 1960, the founder Henry Ford appointed McNamara president of Ford, the first non-Ford family president in the company's history. However, four months later, he quit the position to accept the job of Secretary of Defense under President Kennedy. As Defense Secretary he
115 applied to the defense budget the same strict standards of effectiveness and efficiency based on data as he had used at Ford.

Secretary of Defense = Defense Secretary 「国防長官」

Nikita Khrushchev 「ニキータ・フルシチョフ」(1894-1971, 書記長在任は1953年から1964年) ソ連第4代最高指導者。スターリンの恐怖政治を暴露し、西側との共存路線をとった。

the U.S.S.R. (The Union of Soviet Socialist Republics) 「ソビエト社会主義共和国連邦」
　　The Soviet Union に同じ。1917年ロシア帝国における十一月革命で誕生した世界最初の社会主義国。1922年正式に成立。ロシア・ウクライナ・白ロシア・エストニア・ラトビア・リトアニア・モルダビア・アゼルバイジャン・アルメニア・グルジア・カザフ・トルクメン・キルギス・ウズベク・タジクの15共和国から構成され、国有企業による「計画経済」で発展を目指した。現ポーランドの港町グダンスクで始まった「連帯運動」（独立労働組合、カトリック信仰、愛国意識の融合した人民運動）を震源として各共和国の独立が進み、1989年11月のベルリンの壁崩壊（東西冷戦と民族分断の象徴だったドイツのベルリンの壁が市民によって平和裏に打ち倒された歴史的事件）、東西ドイツ統一を経て、1991年12月、スラブ系ソ連構成国のロシア、ウクライナ、ベラルーシ3共和国首脳がソ連解体と独立国家共同体（CIS）の創設を決定。中央アジアや外カフカスなどのソ連構成国も合流し、同月21日のCIS正式結成でソ連は解体、消滅した。

以下の質問に日本語で答えなさい。

1. 「キューバ危機」において、誰のどのような見解が、ケネディ大統領をキューバ侵攻回避に導いたか。

2. マクナマラの経歴をまとめよ。

3. 米軍による日本爆撃について、マクナマラはどんな点に疑問を持っているか。2点挙げよ。

4. フォード社の重役に着任後、マクナマラは何をしたか。

5. ケネディ政権下の国防長官となったマクナマラは防衛予算をどうしたか。

73

Unit 12

The Fog of War:

Eleven Lessons from the life of Robert S. McNamara <2>

Anti-Vietnam War Protestors in Washington D.C.

UNIT 12

Get Ready with Vocabulary

I　日本語に相当する英語を選びなさい。

1. 関与	2. 暗殺する	3. 有害である	4. 増強する	5. 権限を与える
_____	_____	_____	_____	_____

6. 方策	7. 植民地入植者	8. 悪化させる	9. 辞任する	10. 装置
_____	_____	_____	_____	_____

device　　　**involvement**　**deteriorate**　**assassinate**　**detrimental**
enhance　　**resign**　　　**authorize**　　**measure**　　**colonizer**

II　日本語に相当するよう、選択肢を使って英語を完成しなさい。

conscientious　　**unilaterally**　　**convince**　　**unanimously**　　**deployment**

1. 軍の配置　　　　　　　　　　**troop** [　　　　　　　　]
2. 全会一致で賛成する　　　　　[　　　　　　　　] **approve**
3. 一方的に力を行使する　　　　**use power** [　　　　　　　　]
4. 同盟国を納得させる　　　　　[　　　　　　　　] **our allies**
5. 努力家で注意深い仕事をする男　**hardworking,** [　　　　　　　　] **man**

75

Reading

Over the Vietnam War

President Kennedy and McNamara, 1962

Who really is to blame for America's extended involvement in the Vietnam War? In the movie *The Fog of War*, we hear two conversations involving McNamara, first with J. F. Kennedy taped in November 1963 and next with L. B. Johnson taped in February 1964. In the first conversation, McNamara and Kennedy are talking about the possibility of pulling out all U.S. advisors from Vietnam within two years. On November the 2nd, a little while before this conversation, the President of South Vietnam, Ngo Dinh

Ngo Dinh Diem, Assassinated, November 2nd, 1963

Diem was murdered in a coup. McNamara says he never saw Kennedy so upset. The CIA either aided the coup or failed to rescue Diem despite direct requests from him. On the 22nd of the same month, Kennedy was assassinated.

In the 2nd conversation, we hear Johnson telling McNamara that withdrawing from South Vietnam is foolish and detrimental. They disagree on the severity of the situation in the country. McNamara says that if the U.S. needs to enhance its military actions as Johnson insists, then the American people should first be educated on the dire circumstances in Vietnam.

pull out = withdraw 「退却させる」

Ngo Dinh Diem → Appendix 参照
coup 「クーデター」

educated = informed in details

Lessons 7 and 8 "Belief and seeing are often both wrong," and "be prepared to reexamine your reasoning"

We also hear Johnson, McNamara, and the joint chiefs
35 discussing what exactly happened in what was later known
as the Gulf of Tonkin incident*, in which a North Vietnamese
patrol frigate purportedly fired torpedoes at the U.S. destroyer
Maddox, and about escalating troop deployments in North
Vietnam. The Gulf of Tonkin incident led to increased
40 involvement of the U.S. in Vietnam, yet both what the
Americans believed happened and saw were wrong. While
McNamara encouraged distinct limitations on deployment,
Johnson and the other joint Chiefs of staff are determined
to increase American troops as the circumstances demand.
45 Against McNamara's advice, Congress almost unanimously
approved the Gulf of Tonkin Resolution, authorizing the
president to "take all necessary measures to repel any armed
attack against the forces of the U.S. and to prevent further
aggression." Thus the U.S. entered the morass of the Vietnam
50 War.

Hindsight shows us how Johnson's White House could not
empathize with the Vietnamese as Kennedy learned to do with
the Soviets. Like many Americans, the White House thought
the Vietnamese were puppets of the communist Chinese,
55 whereas the Vietnamese had been fighting the Chinese for
a thousand years. To the Vietnamese, the Americans were
colonizers just like the French. McNamara reflects that, "The
U.S. saw the conflict in Vietnam as a Cold War battle, but the
people in Vietnam saw it as a civil war." He adds, "Though
60 America is the most powerful nation in the world today, we
should not use power unilaterally. If we cannot convince our
allies of the correctness of our actions, we should reexamine
our reasoning."

patrol frigate 「哨戒艇」
(frigate 「フリゲート」
は通常、駆逐艦より大
きく、巡洋艦より小さ
い)
destroyer 「駆逐艦」

**the Gulf of Tonkin resolu-
ion** 「トンキン湾決議」
米議会は上院 88 対 2、
下院 416 対 0 でベトナ
ム戦争介入の大統領支
持を決議した。
aggression 「侵攻」

Hindsight shows 「ふり
返ればわかる」

Cold War 米ソを中心と
する、第二次世界大戦
後の東西冷戦

allies 「諸同盟国」

The Fog of War: Eleven Lessons from the Life of Robert S. McNamara (2)

Lessons 9 and 10 "In order to do good, you may have to engage in evil," and "never say never."

The tensions between Johnson and McNamara resulted in McNamara's stepping down from his role as Defense Secretary. McNamara holds the belief that responsibility for the Vietnam War lies with the president. He assumes that the situation would not have deteriorated so badly if Kennedy had lived. On the other hand, he refuses to explain why he did not speak out against the war after he resigned. He only states he is sorry for his errors. "Even though we have to engage in evil at times, we must do our best to minimize it." Further he emphasizes that Johnson was responding to the cold war realities of the time involving great risks of nuclear war. The implication is that anyone in the same circumstances may find himself making decisions that involve the killing of many people. Never say never.

step down 「辞任する」

Never say never. 通常、「あきらめるな」という意味だが、ここでは「何が起こるか予想はつかない」ともとれる

The final lesson: "You cannot change human nature."

For Robert McNamara, the phrase "the fog of war" refers to how complex war is and how the human mind is unable to fully comprehend all of the variables at one time, resulting in unnecessary deaths. This is his ultimate defense. He says human nature makes it impossible to end war, for our rationality has limits.

variables 「変数」「変化する諸要素」

Often painted in the press as a cold statistical monster without feeling for the human lives his decisions cost, in this documentary, McNamara comes across as a decent, hardworking, conscientious man.   While those wanting to point blame may be disappointed that this interview gives no hidden information about the wars he engaged in as "chess master," it gives a rare glimpse into the mind of a major policy maker, and shows us how an individual's personality may effect the path a country takes.

come across as ~ 「~という印象を与える」

Tokyo after Being Firebombed

 Errol Morris uses an original interviewing device called the "interrotoron*," which places the viewer in the position of the interviewer. Hence, McNamara stares directly at us as he talks, making direct "eye contact." Although the film takes a seemingly non-judgmental approach, the eye contact creates the effect as if McNamara is confessing directly to us his war crime guilt and the intentions behind his decisions, and thus renders the movie a unique narrative power.

---

the Gulf of Tonkin incident　「トンキン湾事件」
 1964 年 8 月、北ベトナム沖のトンキン湾で北ベトナム軍の哨戒艇が米海軍の駆逐艦に 2 発の魚雷を発射したとされる事件。これをきっかけに、合衆国政府は本格的にベトナム戦争に介入、北爆を開始した。しかし、国防総省国際安全保障局の国際安全保障問題担当次官補のジョン・マクノートンが命じて、レスリー・ゲルブ（後に国務省軍政局長）が中心になってまとめ、ウォンキ国防次官補に提出された、トンキン湾事件に関する極秘文書、通称「ペンタゴン・ペーパーズ」を、1971 年 6 月米紙『ニューヨーク・タイムズ』が入手し、事件は共産主義の拡大を恐れた米政府が仕組んだものであったことを暴露した。

"interrotoron"　「インテルロトロン」
 エロール・モリス監督が生み出したインタヴュー装置。カメラの中に原稿が映し出し、カメラを見ながら原稿を読むことができる「テレプロンプター」という既存の装置の原理を使い、原稿が映し出されるところにインタヴュアーである自分の映像を映し、インタヴューを受ける人のアイコンタクトを確保することによって、「映画を見る人に向けられたドラマティックな告白」という感覚を実現した。

The Fog of War: Eleven Lessons from the Life of Robert S. McNamara (2)

以下の質問に日本語で答えなさい。

1. ケネディとマクナマラの会話の内容はどんなものだったか。また、ジョンソンとマクナマラは、会話でそれぞれどう述べたか。

2. 「トンキン湾事件」および「トンキン湾決議」とはそれぞれどのようなものか。

3. ベトナム戦争が本格化する前、アメリカはベトナムをどう見ていたか。ベトナム人はアメリカをどう見ていたか。

4. マクナマラの見解にジョンソンの擁護が見られるとすれば、どう述べて擁護しているか。

5. この映画に「一種の語りの力」を与えているのはどんな装置か。

Appendix

Units 1-2

Oil Factor

「石油という要因」「石油のなすこと」。映画 Oil Factor が描くようなアメリカの動きにいたるまでの、世紀をまたいだ石油争奪と価格をめぐる駆け引きの動きをおさえておこう。

▶第二次大戦後まで◀

アメリカでは 1850 年代に石油探索が始まり、1860 年代、ロックフェラーがスタンダード石油の支配権を握るところから石油業界の躍進が始まった。彼は石油精製事業から始めて利益独占を目的にトラストを形成し、19 世紀後半にはアメリカの石油市場の 85%を支配した。一方 1870 年代からロシアのバクーで石油採掘が本格的化し、鉄道敷設とタンカーの登場、そしてスエズ運河の開通で輸出が可能となると、ここからアメリカ、ロシア、ヨーロッパ勢による石油戦争が始まる。

20 世紀初頭には車の普及で石油の需要が増大することは予測されていた。アメリカではスタンダード石油トラストへの風当たりが徐々に強くなり、ついに 1909 年に反トラスト訴訟でトラストの解体命令が下される。このころオランダのロイヤルダッチ社の興亡やロシアの政治的混乱で石油開発に停滞が見られるなか、外国資本によるイランでの石油採掘が始まった。第一次世界大戦では、イギリスとドイツの対立の中、イギリスでは石油が艦隊に広い行動範囲とスピード、短時間の燃料補給という利点を与えると考え、対するドイツ艦隊は石炭を燃料にしており、本国の外に補給基地がないため行動範囲に制約されて終戦を迎えることになった。イギリスの成功は戦争における石油の重要性を明らかにした。

1920 年代、アメリカで自動車が大量生産されガソリン消費が拡大する。石油の重要性が世界で認識される中、無秩序な採掘や、新たにメキシコなどの中南米やソ連でも採掘が始まり、供給過多となって価格競争が発生。しかしアメリカは生産量を抑制し国内の価格低下を防いだ。世界各地で、石油利権の確保のための提携や対立がみられるようになり、中東の産油国でも、外国政府と石油利権に関する提携が模索され対立も生じた。

1930 年代、日本が対中戦争を始めた背景には、日本の急激な成長への警戒から日本への石油資源供給が制約されたことがある。石油補給ができなくなったことは日本の敗戦の要因で、石油は日本のアキレス腱だと認識された。

第二次大戦末期ごろ、アメリカ国内の油田の枯渇が心配される一方、中東油田の発見が続き、多くの国が中東に漸近。中東石油が世界の重心を動かすようになる。中東における石油利権の争いの中で、サウジアラビアをはじめ産油国の上層部は石油会社に利益を要求するようになり、結果、石油会社は産油国と利益を折半することになる。サウジアラビアとアラコムの 1950 年の協定がその分水嶺であった。

▶オイルショックまで◀

　1950年、当時世界の40%の石油を産出していたイランで革命が起きるが失敗におわり、シャー（国王）の復帰とともに後ろだてとなるアメリカ石油会社がイランに進出する。

　1956年エジプトのナセル大統領がアスワン＝ハイダム建設費の財源とするためスエズ運河の国有化を発表。反発したイギリスがフランスと共にエジプトを攻撃し、第2次中東戦争（スエズ戦争）が起きる。スエズ運河は1869年に営業を開始、1875年にイギリスが買収して以来、スエズ運河会社がその利益をイギリスやフランスの株主に分配し、エジプトにはごくわずかな利益しかもたらしていなかった。このスエズ危機は以後の石油輸送に影響した。パイプラインの増設や、さらに日本の造船技術が大型タンカーを可能にしたこともあり、石油会社は喜望峰周りのタンカーでの運送の道をとった。

　中東ではイタリアや日本などが新しいプレーヤーとして登場し、一方、中東や中南米の産油国は外国に流出する石油の利益を減らそうとした。こうした中で、西欧の石油会社に対抗するため、産油国同士の連携が産まれてきた。

　1960年、スタンダード石油が一方的に石油公示価格引き下げると、対抗するためOPECが創出される。ただちに成果は見えなかったが、1970年代に入り、世界の工業発展による急激な消費増によって、石油は供給過剰状態から供給不足状態へとなる。産油国はOPECを通じて公示価格引き上げに動いた。さらに1973年の第4次中東戦争では、石油の禁輸が産油国の武器として使われた。禁輸は停戦後も続いて先進工業国にパニックを引き起こした。こうした中で日本が親アラブ政策をとるなど、政治にも影響を与える。禁輸政策によりOPECの石油価格の決定力は絶対的なものとなった。

▶オイルショック後◀

　石油禁輸による第一次石油ショックに対し、日本は徹底的な省エネ策を進め、フランスも省エネと同時に核燃料開発を進めた。またイギリスの北海油田など中東以外での石油資源開発の推進といったさまざまな措置がとられた。

　1979年、イランでイスラム革命が起こり、親米のパーレビ国王体制が倒され、革命派の学生たちが「スパイの巣窟」と名付けたテヘランのアメリカ大使館を占拠、米外交官ら61人を人質にして444日間も幽閉した。このできごとは第2次オイルショックを引き起こし、再び石油の大幅な不足をもたらした。続く1980年のイラン・イラク戦争はさらなる石油価格の高騰を予測させたが、先進国は石油の買いあさり中止を申し合わせて価格高騰を防ぎ、OPECの価格決定力を弱めることに成功した。

　1980年代には、石油消費効率化とともに、OPEC以外の地域での油田開発が進んだ。OPECは減産により価格維持を図ったが、石油の市場取引が進み、石油業界が再編される中で石油は徐々に一般商品化する。1980年代半ばには、石油価格の低下への価格競争が始まった。OPECの対抗措置も効力を発せず、価格の上昇には繋がらなかった。その後、中国などの台頭で石油需要が増えたうえ世界的な金融緩和で金余り状態となり、原油価格は鰻登りとなったが、近年はシェールガスの増産供給やイランの石油増産の見込みなどで価格の下落傾向が経済不安の一因となることもある。

Appendix

Unit 3

teachers' unions

　「教員組合」。アメリカ合衆国には大きく 2 つの組合、AFT（アメリカ教員連盟）と NEA（全米教育協会）がある。AFT は教員の生活を守る労働条件を重視して、教員評価についても全米的な問題として現実的に対応していく方針であるが、NEA はこれを各州に委ねて州レベルで取り組ませる方針で、法廷に教員評価問題を持ち込む地域も出ている。教員評価について AFT のウィンガーテン委員長は、「授業観察の結果、教員自身の自己評価、諸発表、レッスンプラン、生徒の学習状況などを総合的に評価して決める」としている。また「教員の勤務評定に生徒の学習成績を反映させること」については、単純な前年度との比較ではなく、今、実際の授業でどのように向上したかに重点をおく」とする。こうして教員の勤務評定を総合的な基準を与えることで教員のみならず教育関係管理職、親なども満足させると期待しているとの見解示したが、勤務評定の資料公表には反対している。一方 NEA 各支部の見解は統一されておらず、有力なカリフォルニア、ニュージャージー、フロリダ支部は「少しでもメリットペイ（学生の成績などが給与に反映する）がある勤務評定には断固反対」を示している。

　チャーター・スクールについても両者で見解が分かれる。AFT は 2010 年のシアトルにおける年次大会にビル・ゲイツをゲストとして招き、「チャーター・スクールは真に教育改革に値するような成果を挙げている。これは教育における大きな変化であり、その努力は生徒の成績にそのまま反映されている」という彼のスピーチを大多数の組合員が受け入れる姿勢であった。一方 NEA はニューオリンズの年次大会に前教育副長官のダイアナ・ラヴィッチを招き、その「チャーター・スクールは公立学校より良い成績をとっていない」という報告に拍手喝さいをおくった。ラヴィッチは教育評論家として教員の勤務評定にメリットペイを導入することに反対しており、理由として、生徒の成績スコアについて教員の結果責任はせいぜい 10% ～ 20% にすぎず、生徒の家庭の収入という要因が大きく働いていて 60% の割合を占めていること、しかも教員はクラスを選ぶことはできず指定される立場であることを上げている。教育とは長期に全人格的に影響する活動であり、一年間の生徒のスコアだけで「高い指導効果を挙げた」とか「平均より劣る」などと評定することは奇妙であるとも述べている。（『デイリーニュース』　ニューヨーク版、2010 年 8 月 19 日号、10 月 25 日号）

83

Unit 6

Manhattan project

　「マンハッタン計画」。原爆製造のためにアメリカが第二次世界大戦中に実施した計画。原爆製造に関わった研究者としてアインシュタインの名がしばしば言及されるが、広島と長崎への原爆投下までの研究の流れは以下のとおり。

　1938年ウラン（U235）の核分裂反応がドイツのベルリンにおいて、O・ハーンとF・シュトラスマンによって発見され、その内容が1939年にはアメリカに伝わった。当時すでにカリフォルニアのE・ローレンスのもとで最新鋭の粒子加速器サイクロトロンがつくられており、ただちにウランの核反応の詳細が調べられた。1940年には、サイクロトロンを使った連鎖核分裂反応をおこすプルトニウム（Pu239）の生成にUCバークレーのG・シーボーグ等らが成功したが、プルトニウムの発見・合成はすでに兵器開発の一環とされ、公表されなかった。そして1941年には、元マサチューセッツ工科大学副学長V・ブッシュが科学研究開発部長になり、原爆の本格的開発をめざしたマンハッタン計画の実施が決定された。

　このとき、ウラン（U235）とプルトニウム（Pu239）の二つを用いる原爆製造方法が想定されたが、天然ウランにおいては核分裂反応を起こすU235は0.7％しかなく、原爆としてU235を使うためには純度を90％以上にする必要がある。これがウラン濃縮である。大量にウラン濃縮をするにはガス拡散法やサイクロトロン用に開発された巨大磁石を使う（電磁分離法）などの大規模施設が必要で、テネシー州オークリッジに濃縮施設が建設された。他方、プルトニウムの場合は、E・フェルミやL・シラードによって考案された原子炉を使うことが構想された。原子炉（黒鉛炉）の中で天然ウランを「燃焼」させ、天然ウラン中のU235を核分裂させて中性子を発生させ、中性子がU238にあたってPu239に転換になる反応を利用してプルトニウムを生産させるという方法である。シカゴ大学に世界最初の原子炉CP-1（シカゴパイル）がつくられ、1941年12月には連鎖反応が確認されたのち、人口の少ないワシントン州ハンズフォードにプルトニウム生産炉が建設された。つまり原子炉は、原爆製造のためのプルトニウム生産の装置であった。

　こうして生産されたウランとプルトニウムを原爆に製造する施設として、1943年、ニューメキシコ州にロスアラモス研究所が作られ、所長に理論物理学者のオッペンハイマーが就任。1945年7月16日、ロスアラモス南方のアラゴモードでプルトニウム原爆の核実験（トリニティ実験）が行われ、実験の仕上げとして8月6日に広島にウラン原爆が、8月9日には長崎にプルトニウム原爆が投下された。（平田光司「マンハッタン計画の現在」（歴史学研究会編『震災・核災害の時代と歴史学』、青木書店、2012年）

　2015年、京都大学の未整理資料から、第二次世界大戦中に日本軍も原爆の開発を急いでいたことを示す書類が見つかった。原子力国家である日本は今、年間三百数十回に及ぶIAEAの査察を受け入れている。

Unit 11

General Curtis LeMay

「カーティス・ルメイ将軍」。第二次世界大戦時、爆撃任務の高い中止率へのルメイの対応について、映画中でマクナマラはこう証言している。「指揮官の一人にカーティス・ルメイというB-24部隊を指揮する大佐がいた。彼は私が戦中に出会った者の中で最も優れた戦闘指揮官だった。しかし彼は異常に好戦的で、多くの人が残忍だとさえ思った。ルメイは（爆撃機の空爆任務の中断率に関する調査で、高い中止率の原因は隊員が撃墜を恐れてこじつけの理由で任務放棄しているに過ぎないと結論づけたマクナマラの）報告書を受けた後、命令をだした。『これから全ての任務において自分が先陣の爆撃機に搭乗する。今後は出撃した全ての爆撃機が攻撃目標まで到達する。これを成し遂げないものは全員軍法会議にかけ処分する。』任務中止率は瞬く間に低下した。彼はそういう類の指揮官だった。」

Curtis LeMay

"One of the commanders was Curtis LeMay - Colonel in command of a B-24 group. He was the finest combat commander of any service I came across in war. But he was extraordinarily belligerent, many thought brutal. He got the report. He issued an order. He said, 'I will be in the lead plane on every mission. Any plane that takes off will go over the target, or the crew will be court-martialed.' The abort[SIC] rate dropped overnight. Now that's the kind of commander he was."

1945年9月20日、ルメイは「戦争はソ連の参戦や原爆がなくても、（終戦日から）2週間以内には終わっていただろう。原爆投下は戦争終結とはなんら関係もない」と答えた。1988年の自書では、「原爆を使用せずに戦争を終わらせることができたとしても、私は、原爆投下は賢明な決定だったと思う。なぜなら原爆投下が降伏交渉を早めたから」と著し、原爆投下は上陸作戦前に日本を降伏させ、100万のアメリカ兵の命を救った、という米政府の公式説明を支持している。

冷戦時代は当時の主力機であるボーイングB-52爆撃機や超音速爆撃機の開発を指揮。「我々は朝鮮の北でも南でも全ての都市を炎上させた。我々は100万以上の民間人を殺し数百万人以上を家から追い払った」と語った。（荒井信一『空爆の歴史—終わらない大量虐殺』岩波新書 p.190）

1964年、日本の航空自衛隊の育成に協力があったとして勲一等旭日大綬章を受勲。当時、佐藤総理は「今はアメリカと友好関係にあり、功績があるならば過去は過去として功に報いる」とした。通例、勲一等の授与は天皇が直接手渡す"親授"となるが、昭和天皇はそうはせず、自衛隊航空幕僚長が入間基地で授与した。後に『NHK特集 東京大空襲』（1978年3月9日初回放送）における取材で、戦争責任についての問いに対してルメイはその勲章を見せて答えとしている。その後、1965年2月7日、ベトナム戦争で北爆を開始するさい、「ベトナムを石器時代に戻してやる」と豪語したと記録される。

Unit 12

the Vietnam War

　「ベトナム戦争」。その原因は少なくとも第二次世界大戦前後に遡る。当時ベトナムはフランス領インドシナ連邦としてフランスの植民地だったが、ヨーロッパで大戦が勃発し、1940年6月にはフランスはドイツに降伏。日本軍がフランス領インドシナ連邦に進駐することになる。その日本が最終的に敗北し、1945年9月、北部にホー・チ・ミン率いるベトナム独立同盟がベトナム民主共和国を樹立し、独立を宣言する。この独立を認めたくない戦勝国、特にフランスは南部に傀儡政権を建国。北ベトナムと争うことになる（第1次インドシナ戦争）。8年続いたこの戦いはフランスの敗北に終わり、1954年7月、ジュネーヴ協定により北緯17度線を境にしてベトナムは分断される。南ベトナムにはアメリカを後ろ盾としたゴ・ディン・ジエム（次項目参照）が大統領となり国名をベトナム共和国とするが、政権内部は汚職まみれで、国民の大多数を占める農民の支持を得られなかった。機を見た北ベトナムは、武力による統一を試みて南ベトナム開放民族戦線（ベトコン）を結成し、内戦が始まる。

　1961年アメリカ大統領ケネディは、ソ連が後ろ盾となっている北ベトナムが勝利すればドミノ倒しのように東南アジアが次々と共産化する、と恐れて、南ベトナムに4000名の特殊部隊を派遣することを決意。その後1964年のトンキン湾事件を機に直接介入に踏み切る。1965年、北ベトナムに255万トンもの爆弾を落とす大規模な爆撃を行った。（太平洋戦争で日本が受けた爆弾の量は13万トン。）しかしソ連などの社会主義陣営からの支援とジャングルでのゲリラ戦で北ベトナム軍はアメリカ軍を撃破する。アメリカは最大時には54万もの兵力を投入したが、ジャングル内では物資や食料の供給が困難で、実際に最前線で戦ったのは3割ほどだったこと、またアメリカ国内でベトナム反戦運動が起きたことも敗北の要因である。アメリカ軍を引き上げたあと南ベトナムは抵抗のしようもなく1975年4月30日、南ベトナム大統領官邸は南ベトナム開放民族戦線によって占領され10年続いたベトナム戦争は終わりを告げた。

Ngo Dinh Diem

　「ゴ・ディン・ジエム」。ベトナム共和国（南ベトナム）初代大統領（1901年–1963年11月2日）。在任は1955年10月から。

　1945年、日本軍がベトナムの実権を握った時に出国し、日本が敗戦してベトナムがフランスの植民地に戻った後も亡命生活を送ったが、1954年ジュネーヴ協定締結直前にサイゴンに帰国し元首となる。反共主義者であったため、東南アジアでの共産主義拡大を懸念するアメリカのバックアップを受け、

Ngo Dinh Diem,
1st President of South Vietnam

ジュネーヴ協定に基づく南北統一総選挙を拒否してベトナム民主共和国（北ベトナム）への対決色を強め、弟のゴ・ディン・ヌーに秘密警察と軍特殊部隊を掌握させて、国内の共産主義者らを弾圧した。

1961 年、大統領に就任したケネディは、フルブライト上院外交委員会委員長に、「南ベトナムとラオスの支援のため米軍を南ベトナムとタイに送る」と通告。この決定の根拠を得るため、ジョンソン副大統領とマクナマラ国防長官をベトナムに派遣し視察に当たらせた。「ジエム大統領は国民から乖離しており、取り巻きが悪い」とジョンソンは報告している。カトリック教徒であるジエムは、仏教徒を弾圧し、高名な僧侶が米大使館前で抗議の焼身自殺をする事件がおきたが、ジエムの実弟ヌーの妻がそれを「単なる人間バーベキューよ」とコメントするといったことがあり、ケネディは一族への不信を募らせた。1963 年 8 月、ケネディが特命全権大使として南ベトナムに送り込んだヘンリー・ロッジ Jr. は、ヌー秘密警察長官の更迭を求めるべくジエムに会見を申し込んだが拒否される。このとき、もしジエムが拒否したら「（アメリカは）ジエム自身を保護できない可能性に直面する」と警告せよ、とケネディの指示が出ていた。まもなくベトナム軍内の反ジエム勢力によってクーデターが計画され、状況は南ベトナム軍事援助司令部を経由してケネディ政権にも逐次報告されるようになっていた。11 月 2 日、ジエムとヌーは反乱部隊によって政権の座から下ろされ、逃げ込んだサイゴン市チョロン地区のカトリック教会の前にて、反乱部隊の装甲兵員輸送車の中で殺害された。

ケネディがどこまで反ジエムのクーデターに関与、支持していたのかについては今も議論が分かれている。マクナマラとロッジ大使は「ケネディ大統領は、ジエムに対するクーデターの計画があることを知りながら、あえて止めなかった」と、ケネディが黙認したことを証言している。ジエム殺害の報告を受けたケネディは、「このクーデターにアメリカは関係していない」との声明を出すよう指示した。